Return and Rest

A Study in Isaiah 30

Elizabeth Renicks

Return and Rest: A Study in Isaiah 30

ISBN: 979-8-9994354-0-8

Welcome

Dear Reader,

I am so delighted you found your way to this Bible Study. I pray God uses it to strengthen your relationship with Him in ways that exceed your expectations. Welcome to an adventure into more of Him! May your study be fruitful and your heart be stirred to love Him more.

What you are holding in your hands is both a deep dive into God's Word and an opportunity for self-reflection and contemplation. As such, you may find the pacing of six chapters with five lessons a week of study to be intense. As presented, the material is a brisk, in-depth study. It is certainly doable as a six-week study, but it can also be accomplished at a slower pace.

God is not in a hurry. There will likely be places He calls you to linger with Him. I encourage you to feel the freedom to do that as you need to, especially if you are working through this material on your own. If you are studying with a group, you may want to discuss ahead of time the option of completing the lessons over a longer period.

One option is to complete the study over twelve weeks instead of six, taking two weeks to complete each chapter of the study. If you choose that approach, I recommend the following pace, which calls for three days of study per week:

- During the first week in a chapter, read the introductory page and complete Lessons One through Three.
- During the second week in that same chapter, complete Lessons Four and Five, then do the prayer and promise page as a separate lesson.

A leader's guide and small group discussion questions for both a six-week and twelve-week approach are available here:

Welcome to this space where I pray you encounter more of Him,

Elizabeth

Introduction

Intimacy is an Investment

We are created for intimacy with God. The Bible teaches we can only be fully whole through union with Him. The first step to intimacy with God is accepting His invitation to personal relationship with Jesus Christ for the forgiveness of your sins. This study presumes you have already taken that step. If you have not, stop right here and make that your pursuit. If you have received Jesus as Lord of your life, keep reading. The invitation we will explore over the next weeks is for you!

Isaiah 30 is one small chapter in a much larger story, but it is filled with God's redemptive work in the lives of His people. As you investigate this chapter of Scripture, you will encounter direction for increased intimacy with your Creator and the lover of your soul. Let us begin with the end in mind: the goal of this study (or of any Christian discipleship) is for you to have increased union with God. Jesus prayed for this very thing before His crucifixion (John 17).

The Bible reveals many obstacles to union with Christ. A saying that dates to the Middle Ages identifies three of them as "the world, the flesh, and the devil." The Bible affirms all three. It teaches we live in a fallen, broken world. We are born with a sin nature longing to put us instead of God on the throne of our lives. We also have an enemy who seeks to destroy our relationship with God.

In *Mere Christianity,* C.S. Lewis describes it this way: "Enemy occupied territory—that is what this world is. Christianity is the story of how the rightful king has landed, you might say landed in disguise, and is calling us to take part in a great campaign of sabotage."[1]

Amid this backdrop, we have a loving God who calls us to intimacy with Him despite all opposition. Isaiah 30 is filled with this theme. God is powerful enough to pull off what we cannot: overcoming all that seeks to separate us from Him.

Cultivating intimacy with God is a lifetime transformation project, and God is the one doing the transforming. Sanctification is the theological name for this process. God grows us

---

[1] Lewis, C. S. *Mere Christianity: A Revised and Amplified Edition, with a New Introduction, of the Three Books Broadcast Talks, Christian Behaviour, and Beyond Personality.* HarperOne, 2009.

up in Him just as a parent helps a child mature and grow (Ephesians 5:1, 8-10). His Spirit brings us freedom and transforms us from glory to glory (2 Corinthians 3:17-18).

But we are called to cooperate with this work by keeping in step with the Spirit (Galatians 5:16-25). This involves no small amount of surrender. The joys and delights of intimacy with Christ are treasure worth pursuing, just like the pearl and the treasure hidden in a field found in Jesus' parables (Matthew 13:44-46).

These are some of the things we will explore in this study.

Why Isaiah?

Why an Old Testament passage to explore intimacy with God? And why a book of prophecy when prophecy has a reputation for being hard to understand?

Studying the Old Testament honors the important truth that the Bible is one story. We do well not to ignore the foundational testament. What we call the Old Testament was the only Scripture that existed when Jesus walked the earth. His words indicate He valued it (Matthew 5:17; Luke 24:44-45). New Testament writers valued these texts as well (Romans 1:1-2, 15:3; 2 Timothy 3:15-16). We can turn to Isaiah 30 with firm expectation of finding lessons and truths to significantly shape us and our relationship with God today.

Additionally, learning to dig into the riches of a prophetic text is a great skill. Such a text forces us to slow down, to pay attention to context, to look closely at terms and literary structures that are not as straightforward as we might like. In other words, we have a hard time skimming such text. Slowing down might just grow our attention span in ways we desperately need.

The first couple of lessons may feel a bit demanding if you are not familiar with Old Testament history. It might not feel easy to "enter in" confidently, but nothing is too hard for God. He will help you as you invite Him to lead your study. If needed, consult a study Bible or commentary for additional help. Online resources such as blueletterbible.org or studylight.org offer a selection of commentaries.

A Little History

The prophecies in Isaiah were written generations after the Kingdom of Israel divided into two nations (1 Kings 12, 2 Chronicles 10-12). The Northern Kingdom, whose capital was eventually established at Samaria, was made up of ten of the original twelve tribes. In the Bible, the Northern Kingdom is typically referred to as Israel to distinguish it from the Southern Kingdom of Judah. Made up of just two tribes, Judah and Benjamin, the Southern

Kingdom's capital was Jerusalem. The Southern Kingdom is most often referred to in Scripture by the name Judah.

Isaiah lived in Jerusalem, and his prophecies were largely directed to Judah. For the purposes of this study, the term Judah will be used to indicate the people addressed in Isaiah 30. This distinguishes them from the Northern Kingdom, which will be designated as Israel.

Features of This Study

Each chapter of this study has a specific theme and is divided into five lessons which explore the theme in more detail.

Lessons for each chapter begin with an overview page featuring the theme, a Key Idea, and a Key Verse. Together these give a preview and introduction to what you will study.

The lessons guide you through study of Isaiah 30 and other passages of Scripture. Each lesson starts with a prayer to read aloud as you begin. Often, lessons will include reflection questions or personal assessment opportunities. Space is provided to record thoughts. If you are studying with a group, weekly meeting times will give an opportunity to share your insights or discuss any questions that arise as you study. A small group discussion guide is available here:

At the end of each chapter is a closing page, featuring a short summary of the lessons, a Key Practice, a Key Promise, and a prayer. The Key Practice invites self-reflection and engagement with truths you are learning. The Key Promise in each chapter is a Scripture with a promise related to the chapter's topic. These are wonderful verses to memorize.

You'll also find the full text of Isaiah 30 in the English Standard Version at the back of the study.

My prayer is that you will find a deeper love for God and receive more of His love as you study these next weeks. He longs to be gracious to you (Isaiah 30:18).

General Information on Isaiah

Isaiah is nearly the longest book in the Bible, second only to the Psalms in number of chapters. The prophecies of Isaiah are primarily to the Southern Kingdom of Judah during the time of the divided kingdom in Israel's history.

According to Isaiah 1:1, Isaiah prophesied during the reigns of Judean kings Uzziah, Jotham, Ahaz, and Hezekiah. No clear date is available for the exact beginning and end of Isaiah's ministry, but it is generally thought he ministered from 740-690 BC.

Prophetic books operate on several levels, with warnings for the prophet's own time, warnings of near future events (such as impending captivity), and prophecies about distant future events, such as those about Jesus the Messiah. For present-day readers, all but some of the far-distant events have already happened.

For this reason, we must read prophetic books carefully. Isaiah delivered many messages concerned specifically with his own era. We can, however, derive lessons from such writings when we encounter parallel situations in present times. This study will take that approach, looking at truth for today from this ancient spokesperson of God.

The book of Isaiah has two major portions: chapters 1-39 are concerned with events relating to Assyria and themes of judgment and warning; chapters 40-66 are concerned with the comfort of God and focus on rescue and return from Babylon. The message of Isaiah is united in the way it points to both a holy and a merciful God.

Isaiah 30 is in the section of the book primarily concerned with warnings and promises related to events in Judah during Isaiah's lifetime. While a major focus is warning and judgment, chapter 30 reveals a picture of the mercy and compassion of God, who pursues His wayward children with astounding offers of presence, protection, and peace.

Table of Contents

Chapter One: Recognize Circumstances

Key Idea: You can recognize your circumstances and choose how you respond.

Key Verse: "We are hard pressed on every side, but not crushed; perplexed, but not in despair; persecuted, but not abandoned; struck down, but not destroyed."

2 Corinthians 4:8-9 (NIV)

Israelites living in Jerusalem in the years of the divided kingdom had trying times and trust issues. Though exact chronologies for the prophecies are not certain, scholars generally agree. At the time of the events of Isaiah 30, the Northern Kingdom (Israel) had already been conquered by Assyria, and the two tribes of the Southern Kingdom of Judah were under threat.

Just over two decades before the events of Isaiah 30, Judah's wicked King Ahaz had enlisted the Assyrians to attack both Syria and the Northern Kingdom of Israel. Assyria invaded the Northern Kingdom, captured the Israelite capital, Samaria, and took Israelites into captivity (2 Kings 16-17). The Assyrians were interested in dominating the region, not long-term alliances. By the time of Isaiah 30, the Assyrians were set on conquering the Southern Kingdom of Judah too.

The people of Judah did not trust God in the ways described in the key verse above. They trusted more in what they could see, in their fears, and in the resources of stronger neighbors like Egypt. We are not so different at times. We all face hard things. The question is: What choices do we make about the hard things we face? Where do we go for guidance?

In this chapter, we will explore the circumstances of these ancient Judeans and compare them with our own today. Looking at these children of God can teach us about the choices we have in the face of difficult circumstances.

Lesson One: God's Children are Hard Pressed

O loving God, Jesus, Holy Spirit, come into my time of study today. Give me eyes to see and ears to hear what you desire to show me in your Word.

Trying Times

Can you think of a time when you longed for relief from a difficult situation or set of circumstances? Most of us can think of days when we have felt overwhelmed or filled with uncertainty. If you were alive in 2020, you have a very real understanding of what it is like when the world seemingly turns upside down. The context of Isaiah 30 is one of unknowns, a certain amount of chaos, and very real fear. As we turn to this chapter of Scripture, we will learn more about God's grace and His provision for the trying times we all will face.

Context is Important

Any time we come to God's Word, especially when looking for guidance and instruction, it is important to be grounded in the context of what we read. A good way to discover the context of any passage is to consider the circumstances in which the text was written.

As mentioned in the introduction, the prophecies of Isaiah 30 were directed to the nation of Judah during the divided kingdom. During this period, the Assyrian Empire dominated much of the region. Israel's capital, Samaria, had been conquered by Assyria several decades earlier. In Isaiah 30, God is speaking through Isaiah to Judah, whose capital was Jerusalem. In the face of increasing threats, Judah's leadership is seeking a military alliance with Egypt.

Read Isaiah 30:1-5. Write what you find about what Judah is seeking and how God views their plans.

A Physical Threat and Financial Enslavement

By the time of God's words in Isaiah 30:1, the Assyrians were knocking on the door of Jerusalem. Now ruled by Hezekiah, Judah had become more and more threatened by Assyrian power. Though Jerusalem itself had not yet faced military threat, other well-fortified Judean cities had.

Read 2 Kings 18:13-16. What has happened to the "fortified cities of Judah"?

What is Hezekiah's response (verse 14)?

What does the king of Assyria demand and receive (verses 14-16)?

A very real military threat faces Judah. Though these verses don't reveal a lot of detail, the archaeological record does. The savagery and thoroughness of the assault on the cities of Judah is well attested to, especially the battle of Lachish. After placing some 46 strong cities of Judah under siege and destroying even more villages, the armies of Assyria have now turned their eyes to the capital Jerusalem itself.[2]

To stave off potential attack, Judah had worked out with Assyria what we might call a bribery agreement. Assyria accepting "financial tribute" from a militarily weaker nation was a common "negotiating" tactic. As with all bribes, however, the payee usually gets pressed for more than they have. Eventually, the Assyrians came demanding more.

Taunting and Shaming

Read 2 Kings 18:17-21. Who is speaking in verse 19?

What is the message he has for Judah's King Hezekiah?

Who does the Assyrian spokesman taunt Hezekiah for relying on?

---

[2] Anderson, Clive, and Brian Edwards. *Evidence for the Bible*. Day One Publications, 2018. Pages 65-75.

These circumstances are the backdrop of the opening verses of Isaiah 30. In the face of Assyrian threats, Judah has sought an alliance with Egypt. This is met with contempt by the Assyrian representatives. They want Judah to keep paying tribute to their king, so they taunt the representatives of Judah's King Hezekiah.

Psychological Warfare and Terror

Read 2 Kings 18:26-35. Who are the three representatives of King Hezekiah (verse 26)?

What do they ask of the Assyrian Rabshakeh (verse 26)?

Why do you think they ask this?

What is the response of Rabshakeh (verse 27)?

Summarize Rabshakeh's message found in verses 28-35.

The Assyrian spokesman not only taunts and shames the representatives of Judah for seeking an alliance with Egypt, but he then goes after their trust in God. Assyria belittles the idea of any god standing up to their military might. Even more, Rabshakeh makes sure to speak so the people of Judah, not just political representatives, hear his message. He declares Assyria has Judah backed into a corner and suggests no real help is coming. The only option, he says, is for the people to surrender to Assyria.

Read Isaiah 30:1-2. What role do you think fear played in the actions of God's people?

Read Matthew 4:8-10. What is the temptation offered to Jesus?

Compare the Matthew 4:8-10 exchange with the one depicted in 2 Kings 18:31-35. How are they similar?

How are they different?

Present day headlines are a tangle of threats and ever-shifting alliances, but just a brief glimpse at history shows there is nothing new under the sun. Physical threats, economic threats, taunting, shaming, accusation, and mental warfare are still the battles we can face in our day-to-day lives. The enemy of our souls wants us to live in fear.

Just as the faith of God's children was severely tested in the years of Hezekiah's reign, our faith can be severely tested today, often in similar ways. Here is God's word to another, earlier group of Old Testament people who were also hard pressed on every side—the Israelites fleeing Egypt with their backs up against the wall of the Red Sea:

> And Moses said to the people, "Fear not, stand firm, and see the salvation of the LORD, which he will work for you today. For the Egyptians whom you see today you shall never see again. The LORD will fight for you, and you have only to be silent." (Exodus 14:13-14, ESV)

Lesson Two: Slowing Down to See

O loving God, Jesus, Holy Spirit, come into my time of study today. Give me eyes to see and ears to hear what you desire to show me in your Word.

Pay Attention with Three Passes

Today we will look through the first seventeen verses of Isaiah 30. This is a way of slowing down to attend to different things and cultivating eyes to see details better. We will read these verses several times, each time with a different, specific focus. I encourage you to use the ESV text on pages 129-130 for this exercise.

First Pass: What Do I See?

Read Isaiah 30:1-17. On this readthrough, just pay attention to what you find interesting. Have in mind the questions: "What do I notice?" or "What do I see?" Make note of what stands out or any questions you have.

Second Pass: Defining Terms and Structure

Read the same passage again slowly. This time, identify any words you may need to define. Make a list and look up definitions for any unfamiliar terms.

On this reading, also notice the structure of these seventeen verses by paying attention to the speaker and the recipient of the words. The structure might be harder to see in different translations, so using the ESV will help here. God is the speaker starting in verse 1.

To whom is He speaking?

Does He change to whom He is speaking? If so, where?

God speaks to His "stubborn children" living in Judah beginning in verse 1. In verses 1-5, God speaks directly to them, then talks about them in verses 6-7. At verse 8 is a shift. God begins speaking directly to Isaiah. In verses 12-17, God returns to directly addressing Judah.

Compare what God says to Judah in verses 1-7 with His words to Isaiah in verses 8-11. How are they similar?

How are they different?

How are God's words in verses 12-17 like His words in the other sections?

How do they differ?

Third Pass: Relationships

On this last readthrough, pay attention to relationships you notice. There are several ways to do this:

- Look at relationships between Judah and various parties mentioned in the passage (Egypt, Pharaoh, Seers, Prophets, God Himself).
- Take note of any cause-and-effect relationships stated within the passage.
- Observe relationships between words or phrases. Notice any synonyms and repetition within these verses.

Wrap up this lesson by noting any themes or any other new information you have gleaned by slowing down to pay closer attention.

Don't be concerned if you have unresolved questions or even some confusion as you end this lesson. Being attentive to detail usually opens the door to more questions than answers at first, and that is just fine. We will learn more as we go. Trust God to lead you to what He wants you to see and hear as we study.

Lesson Three: Judah Takes a Wrong Path

O loving God, Jesus, Holy Spirit, come into my time of study today. Give me eyes to see and ears to hear what you desire to show me in your Word.

Judah Makes Poor Choices

In Lesson One, we read about the Assyrians taunting Judah about two different sources of outside help: Egypt (2 Kings 18:21) and God (2 Kings 18:30, 33-35). God Himself has something very specific to say about Judah's relationships and the choices they make for help against Assyria.

Read Isaiah 30:1-7. What stands out to you about God's words concerning Egypt?

Read Isaiah 30:8-14. What stands out to you about what God says concerning Judah's view of Him?

In the first seven verses of Isaiah 30, the focus is on the choice to seek help from Egypt; in the next seven verses, the focus is on the choice to completely disregard God. These choices are two different sides of the same coin. Both sets of verses open with God's indictment against His children, followed by a consequence for the choices they are making.

Read Isaiah 30:1-7 again and answer these questions:

How does God describe Judah? (verse 1)	What does He say they have done? (verses 1-2, 6)	What will be the result of this choice? (verses 1, 3-7)

Now do the same with Isaiah 30:8-14:

How does God describe Judah? (verse 9)	What does He say they have done? (verses 10-12)	What will be the result of this choice? (verses 13-14)

In both verses 1 and 9, God refers to those He is speaking to as children. They are described as stubborn, rebellious, faithless, deceptive, deceitful, false, or lying (depending on your translation).

In Isaiah 30:1-7, God says they failed to seek His counsel, made alliances without His Spirit, and will waste their resources seeking help from a worthless ally. The result, He says, will be disappointment, shame, and disgrace.

God asserts in Isaiah 30:8-14 that His children have plugged their ears to His instruction and turned away from Him, seeking an illusion of safety outside His paths. For this, He says, sudden calamity will come with utter destruction.

These are strong accusations and stark warnings. They are entirely warranted. The Northern Kingdom of Israel had taken similar action a few decades before, and the results were not good (2 Kings 17:1-18). By this point in history, God had rescued and forgiven His people many, many times. Through the indictments and warnings in Isaiah 30, God is once again pleading with His children to recognize the folly of their choices.

Blessings, Curses, and Trees

The choice between trusting God or something lesser than Him appears throughout the Bible. Once such place is Deuteronomy 28-30. The setting for these words of Moses is just before God leads His children to the Promised Land. Moses teaches about choices. He contrasts blessings and curses, repentance and forgiveness, and things leading to life or to death. Deuteronomy 29 recounts a renewal of the covenant between God and Israel. This covenant and teachings were the foundation of Jewish life and culture, yet they became diluted and ignored over the years. By the time of Isaiah, the Deuteronomy 28 truths concerning curses for disobedience were coming into full flower.

Scripture teaches that all the choices we have about handling our circumstances are in two categories: God or anything other than Him. Anything other than Him is a lesser god.

More than a hundred years after Isaiah, the prophet Jeremiah ministered to the nation of Judah. Jeremiah's words reveal that a century later, Judah had not made much progress in learning the folly of chasing after lesser gods.

Read a summary of Jeremiah's times found in Jeremiah 16:10-14. What charge does God bring against His children in this passage?

A chapter later, God speaks, employing memorable poetic imagery to illustrate the differences in where we place our trust.

Read Jeremiah 17:5-8. How does God describe the person who trusts in man or his own flesh?

How does God describe the person who trusts in Him?

Compare these two images. How are they similar? How are they different?

Ask God to reveal anything to you that He would like to say through this imagery.

Lesson Four: The Choice to Run or Rest

O loving God, Jesus, Holy Spirit, come into my time of study today. Give me eyes to see and ears to hear what you desire to show me in your Word.

Comparing Choices

The last lesson concluded with a comparison of two trees described in Jeremiah 17. God presents two responses we can have to Him, along with two results. One who trusts in human strength and turns away from the Lord is likened to a shrub in the desert, living in dry places without seeing any good come. One who trusts in the Lord, finding hope and confidence in Him, is described as a fruitful, peace-filled green tree, even in the face of drought and stress.

The people of Judah made plans without God in the face of a frightening Assyrian threat. For this, He takes them to task in Isaiah 30. If you stopped reading at verse 14, you might be tempted to characterize God as angry and vengeful. Context is important. God's mercy and compassion are abundantly clear in the Old Testament, including here.

Read Isaiah 30:15-19. Note anything that stands out to you.

Pursuing Our Own Path

Choices about handling our circumstances are oriented in one of two directions: God's way or the way of lesser gods. Judah has rejected God.

Look again at verses 15-17. God makes an appeal for His wayward children to return to Him. What did they do in response?

According to verse 17, what was the result of this running?

The New Living Translation of verse 17 says: "You will be left like a lonely flagpole on a hill or a tattered banner on a distant mountaintop."

Lonely and tattered. This is the result of running away from God, trying to solve our problems without Him. When we choose to pursue our own path in the wisdom of our own counsel, the result is that we are run ragged and feel alone.

Have you experienced feelings of exhaustion, weariness, or loneliness? How do verses 15-17 speak to those experiences?

Read Jeremiah 17:5-8. Which tree in Jeremiah is similar to what is described in Isaiah 30:16-17?

Returning and Rest

Isaiah 30:15 offers another response to our circumstances: one of returning and resting in God. God offers a call to repentance and forgiveness right on the heels of the list of indictments and warnings in verses 1-14. This rhythm of words of judgment followed by words of reconciliation is seen throughout Old Testament prophecy. What does that say about the heart of God?

Read Isaiah 30:18-19. What does God say about Himself?

What does He want to do for those who come to Him?

Here we see the compassion, mercy, and relational heart of God. He longs to be gracious; He blesses those who wait for Him.

Think back to the trees in Jeremiah 17 and put those images alongside the words of Isaiah 30:15-19. Those who trust in their own strength or in the help of mankind, will end up alone and tattered, much like a shrub struggling to survive in a barren desert. But there is an alternative that leads to life and fruitfulness according to Isaiah 30:15-19. God promises grace and mercy to those who return to Him.

God is Always True to His Word

In Lesson One, we read about the taunting of Judah and the blasphemies of the Assyrian envoy Rabshakeh. Initially Judah paid the bribes required by the Assyrians, but this did not buy lasting peace. What happened next is recorded in 2 Kings 19. Judah's King Hezekiah responded with the type of repentance and rest the Lord urges in Isaiah 30:15.

God was responsive to this return. In the course of events, the armies of Assyria moved steadily to surround Jerusalem. But the Holy One of Israel brought about a great victory over Assyrian King Sennacherib, and He protected the city of Jerusalem. Assyria was defeated by God's own hand, and its haughty King Sennacherib retreated to Ninevah, where he shortly thereafter was murdered by his own two sons (2 Kings 19:20-36). Isaiah 30:30-33 prophesies these events.

In this narrative, we see historical evidence of the compassion of God toward His repentant children, just as He declares to them in Isaiah 30:15 and 18. Throughout history, God offers humanity a choice—trust in Him to meet our need or trust in something less.

The Bottom Line

We can take away lessons from our quick tour of Judah's history:
- God offers us choices, and our choices have impacts and consequences.
- God is faithful to His Word and His character, whether to receive a repentant child or to allow a wayward child to experience consequences of a poor choice.

We are not so different from our forebears in ancient Judah who struggled to trust God during hard times. In the next lesson we will start looking in the mirror.

Lesson Five: Hard Pressed on Every Side

O loving God, Jesus, Holy Spirit, come into my time of study today. Give me eyes to see and ears to hear what you desire to show me in your Word.

We Are Also Hard Pressed

Each of us can relate on some level to the pressures and anxieties the citizens of Judah experienced in the face of threats from the Assyrians. Regardless of our individual circumstances, we all know hardships that create stress, fear, exhaustion, and desperation. It is part of living in a broken world.

Our perspectives on our circumstances greatly affect how we handle them. The Israelites often viewed their circumstances through the lens of thinking "there is no help coming from God." When your life is overwhelming, it is easy to adopt such a lens. The tragic result can be taking matters into your own hands without consulting or trusting God. This is exactly the indictment God made against His children in Isaiah 30:1-17.

Think about your life. Slow down and pay attention. Look at your life from a few different angles, like you did with our text in Lesson Two.

First, look at your calendar and/or your to-do list for the next few weeks. How do these things make you feel? Are you extremely busy? Lonely or bored? Unsure what to do next? Jot down your thoughts here.

Second, consider the realm of your relationships. Think of those closest to you—immediate family or close friendships. Are there connections that are difficult? Next broaden out to other relationships—work life, acquaintances. Do you have places of pressure or difficulty in any of these relationships?

Next, are you facing or have you recently faced a significant emotional event or transition? Some examples: a move, a new job, loss of a friendship or close relationship, illness, a death of one close to you, or other events which represent a major disruption to your "normal" life. List any of those here.

Now, consider your emotional and mental life in different realms. Do you feel stress, anxieties, or worry in any of these arenas? If so, note them.

Physically?

Financially?

Relationally?

Emotionally?

Spiritually?

Other?

We really aren't so distant from our forebears in ancient Jerusalem, are we? Frequently, things tempt us to fear and make us feel vulnerable. We must be aware of the lenses through which we view the events of our lives—especially the ones that are hard, draining, and soul-crushing. Perspective makes a difference.

Fighting Currents or Floating Calmly?

In early 2024, I faced a season of "overwhelm" with our family circumstances. Physical, financial, relational, emotional, and spiritual health were all under strain. Fear, disappointment, and discouragement seemed to be at every turn. We swam in a sea of uncertainty. One morning in prayer, I asked the Lord to show me His perspective on my situation. This is what I wrote in my journal after listening for His response:

"I saw myself treading water, wanting to move gently but pushing hard against the water to stay above it. Jesus then showed me what it looks like to float on my back on top of the water—resting on it confidently, not fighting it to stay afloat, but relaxing on top of it, letting it carry me and my weight.

The water in this picture, I realized, represented circumstances He allows in my life. I can fight against them to try to stay afloat, OR I can lie back on them and be afloat and relax.

So, I relaxed and quit fighting. As I was lying back and starting to float, I sensed Him holding my hand, something He could not do if I used my hands and arms to tread water. He was standing in the deepest of the deep ends and offered a hand to hold as I lay back and rode it out."

I don't have to fear or to fight against the warfare, the brokenness, or the circumstances. He has conquered. He is in control. He offers me a path of floating safely above my circumstances.

Also, He showed me that when I am treading water, my gaze is on the circumstances. I am scanning the horizon or judging the waves, measuring my strength against the challenges. It is exhausting always being on high alert for what might happen. When floating, my eyes are either closed in surrender or they are on the skies, the heavens.

The Spirit impressed on me: "Don't try to fight against the circumstances in your own strength and efforts, trying to get to elusive solid land. Let me carry you above, on top of them—just ride them out with My hand in yours."

After that, God gently reminded me of what He said through Moses to the Israelites when they were stuck between the Egyptian army and the Red Sea.

Read Exodus 14:13-14 and write out verse 14 below.

Hope for Now and For the Future

We live in a broken, war-filled world with some type of threat on every side—just like the Israelites in Isaiah's day. The elusive "solid ground" of perfect and comfortable circumstances are not in this realm. We get only glimpses here. As God's children, of course we long for the "good land" because that is where we belong. God will uphold us until all things are made new and the warring and brokenness is over.

Read Psalm 118:8-16. What do verses 8-9 remind us?

How did the Psalmist address the challenges of his times? (What phrase is repeated in verses 10-12?)

What is said about God and how He meets our challenges in verses 13-16?

Meditate on these words from 2 Corinthians 4:7-9: "But we have this treasure in jars of clay to show that this all-surpassing power is from God and not from us. We are hard pressed on every side, but not crushed; perplexed, but not in despair; persecuted, but not abandoned; struck down, but not destroyed" (NIV).

God is willing to give you the kind of faith and trust that Paul writes about here. Close this lesson by looking over your lists above and offering these hard-pressed places into His care. Isaiah 26:3 offers a lovely promise, showing us what God will do for us: "You will keep in perfect peace all who trust in you, all whose thoughts are fixed on you!" (NLT).

Chapter One Prayer and Promise

As we began our journey through Isaiah 30, we discovered the people of Isaiah's day were faced with tremendous challenges; we discovered their challenges and ours share things in common. Like God's children thousands of years ago, we all will face hard times. We can choose God or choose something less than God to help us through. The best choice is to follow God, but that isn't always the easiest choice. In the coming weeks, we will discover truths and tools to help us choose God and place our trust more deeply in Him.

God speaks, "I am with you" to every one of our hard-pressed places. We must ditch the idea that we can live a perfect, pain-free life on earth. That is not truth; that is a lie the world is selling.

God assures (and reassures) that He is with you, and He cares for your every need. We saw Judah was hard pressed. We are hard pressed. God is faithful, powerful, loving, and unchanging. You can recognize your circumstances and choose how you respond to them.

Key Practice: Ask God to help you identify the circumstances in which you feel the most "hard pressed." Make a list of the concerns you have. Keep adding to it as you need to. Consider those things in light of the Key Promise and prayer below.

Key Promise: "Haven't I commanded you: be strong and courageous? Do not be afraid or discouraged, for the Lord your God is with you wherever you go."

Joshua 1:9 (CSB)

Great and merciful God, thank you for your Word. May I be sustained by it and by your presence in whatever circumstances you have for me. I invite you to guard my heart and mind against speculation about the future, fear, and uncertainty. Reveal to me places I have "run to Egypt" or turned away from you. Meet me there with your grace and love. Help me to make wise choices about where I place my trust. I ask this in Jesus' name.

Notes

Notes

Chapter Two: Respond to Invitation

Key Idea: You can respond to an invitation to an intimate relationship with a powerful, personal God.

Key Verse: "For thus said the Lord GOD, the Holy One of Israel, 'In returning and rest you shall be saved; in quietness and in trust shall be your strength.' But you were unwilling."

Isaiah 30:15 (ESV)

Our last chapter study concerned the life and times of God's children in Jerusalem during the reign of Judah's King Hezekiah. As we discovered, they dealt with some very difficult circumstances. Their first choice concerning how to handle things was not the wisest; Isaiah 30 opens with God taking His children to task for relying on Egypt instead of Him. Judah did not seek Him but sought help elsewhere, "adding sin to sin" (Isaiah 30:1).

Yet, in the midst of a lengthy indictment against His children, God quietly but firmly slips an invitation into their hands: "In returning and rest you shall be saved; in quietness and trust shall be your strength" Isaiah 30:15a (ESV).

Sadly, the next part of the verse records their initial response: "But you were unwilling." God's children made the choice to reject Him and to pursue their own paths. Instead of choosing rest, they chose to run to Egypt; instead of choosing faith in God, they chose flight from Him.

God, however, didn't stop offering a path back to Himself. He invited Judah to return to Him and rest. In this chapter, we will explore this invitation. Because our loving God never changes, this invitation still stands. You have an invitation to an intimate relationship with a powerful, personal God.

Lesson One: What is This Invitation?

O loving God, Jesus, Holy Spirit, come into my time of study today. Give me eyes to see and ears to hear what you desire to show me in your Word.

We Have an Invitation

Most of us have received invitations, whether to an event like a birthday party or a wedding or to join a club or community group. Some people receive so many invitations they cannot possibly accept them all!

What is your reaction when you get an invitation? What do you usually do with it?

At my house, if an invitation to our family comes in the mail, there is a specific spot it goes so I can remember to discuss it with others. If we decide to accept, the event goes onto our calendars. A highly anticipated invitation gets pride of place on the front of the refrigerator.

This chapter will explore the invitation to intimate relationship with the God who created all things, knows us better than we know ourselves, and has the desire and the power to meet all our needs.

Invitations Can Get Lost

When my oldest son graduated from high school, I planned a celebration and sent invitations. Several weeks later family members started asking about plans for his graduation. No one had received their invitations! I was heartsick. I followed up with the post office; nothing could be done to locate them.

I wanted people to share our celebration of his accomplishments. They didn't even get the word. My invitation to celebrate with us got derailed by crazy circumstances.

God's invitation to us also can get derailed by crazy circumstances. Sometimes our lives are so full and busy we feel we cannot do anything but move from one problem to the next. That may be how the residents of Judah felt when they were trying to cope with their hardships by turning to Egypt. Thankfully for them (and us) God is persistent.

God Delivers His Invitation

The context in which God offers invitation to the ancient residents of Jerusalem is significant. The invitation is sandwiched inside a lengthy passage of woes and warnings God made against Judah in the first half of Isaiah 30.

Instead of leaving Judah in a place of condemnation, God voices what has always been on offer: "In returning and rest you shall be saved; in quietness and trust shall be your strength" (Isaiah 30:15a ESV).

Notice the verb tenses in this invitation. They speak of a time to come. "You shall be saved." God isn't saying, "You had your chance and now you've missed it by aligning with Egypt." No. God extends an invitation to restoration even as He calls out His children's wayward behavior.

God knew the Israelites would find themselves attempting to find salvation and strength in other sources besides Him. He also knew He would be ready to receive them back after those times of turning away. He had spoken of it years before.

Read Deuteronomy 4:30-31. What does God say will happen when His children are in trials (verse 30)?

What will God do when they return?

Read 2 Chronicles 7:14. What does God say to His children?

How is it similar to the passage in Deuteronomy 4?

These verses concern returning to God. Each contains the Hebrew word *sub*, which is usually translated as "turn, return, or come back."[3] That same Hebrew word is the root of the word translated *returning* in Isaiah 30:15. The invitation to return to God echoes throughout history.

The words in Deuteronomy were spoken some 700 years before the prophecy of Isaiah 30. The words recorded in 2 Chronicles were spoken at the time of the dedication of Solomon's temple, 250 years before the invitation recorded in Isaiah 30:15. Throughout the years, God is committed to restoration of relationship with His children. God continually

---

[3] "H7725 - Šûḇ - Strong's Hebrew Lexicon (KJV)." *Blue Letter Bible*, www.blueletterbible.org/lexicon/h7725/kjv/wlc/0-1/.

extends an invitation to His children to return to Him, no matter how far they have tried to run, no matter how deeply they have entrusted themselves to others.

An Invitation to You

God knew the challenges, hardships, temptations, and distractions His people would face in the many years following their exodus from Egypt. He also knows all about the current circumstances of your life, the challenges, hardships, temptations, and distractions that you face.

Look back at some of your answers from Chapter One. Where are you hard pressed?

What words describe how you feel when facing difficult circumstances, endless to-do lists, or a crisis?

My list contains words like *overwhelmed, stuck, anxious, uncertain, confused, alone, exhausted,* and *dry.* When I am in even moderately hard times what I want is to be rescued. If your list is anything like mine, there is really good news in Isaiah 30:15. God offers an invitation to salvation and strength that comes in relationship with Him. He is the rescuer.

This invitation hasn't changed. In case you worry that God's Old Testament invitations have an expiration date, consider the words of Jesus. As you read each passage below, write what it invites you to do.

Matthew 11:28

John 7:37

Don't these invitations sound a lot like returning and resting in quiet confidence? Here is one more, extended after Christ's resurrection.

Read Revelation 22:17. What does it invite you to do?

How do these invitations make you feel?

Lesson Two: Who is Inviting?

O loving God, Jesus, Holy Spirit, come into my time of study today. Give me eyes to see and ears to hear what you desire to show me in your Word.

What's in a Name?

All invitations come from a sender. The invitation in Isaiah 30:15 is no different. It comes from "the Lord GOD, the Holy One of Israel." Names had special significance in Old Testament times, serving not only to specify someone, but to reveal an identity and a personality. This is true for God's names as well. Often, however, we breeze past the ways God is named in the Bible. There are fascinating things to learn by looking more closely.

"The Lord GOD, the Holy One of Israel" is a unique expression of who God is. Isaiah 30:15 is the only place in all of Scripture this particular combination of God's names occurs. The juxtaposition reveals several notable things about Him.

Oh LORD, Lord

Most contemporary translations of the Bible include introductory pages explaining how divine names in the text are translated into English. There are differences among various names for God in the Old Testament Hebrew, as well as in the Greek of the New Testament.

Read Exodus 4:10. Look at the word *lord,* which should appear twice in this verse. (If your translation doesn't have it twice, try to find one that does.) What do you notice about how each is printed?

In most translations, the first *lord* in this verse is printed like this: LORD. Notice the second, third, and fourth letters are printed in small capitals. The second *lord* is then printed like this: Lord, with the last three letters in regular lower case.

This variation is one way most English Bible translations make distinctions between two different Hebrew names of God. What is the difference?

Many translations follow this structure: when you see *LORD,* with the small capitals, it signals the Hebrew word being translated is *YHWH.* If you see *Lord* with the regular lower-cased letters, it means the word being translated is the Hebrew *Adonai.*

LORD = YHWH, A Personal, Relational Name

YHWH, what scholars call the tetragrammaton, are four Hebrew letters making up the personal name of God. For reasons lost to history, the exact pronunciation of these Hebrew letters is unknown, though it is often rendered *Yahweh* or *Jehovah*. This is considered the most intimate, personal name of God.

Distilling the entire nature of an infinite God into one succinct name would be impossible. One place we can get more insight into God's name is Exodus 3:13-15. God responds to Moses asking His name with multiple answers.

Read Exodus 3:13-15. What does God call Himself in verse 14?

Find the personal name of God in verse 15 (likely rendered *LORD*). Who else is mentioned in that verse?

What does God say in the last sentence of verse 15?

God reveals Himself in several important ways. In verse 14, he uses a form of the verb "to be"—connecting His personal name in verse 15 (*YHWH* or *LORD*) with the sense of His ever-existing essence. In verse 15, he also connects His personal name to Abraham, Isaac, and Jacob, grounding His identity in relationship. Finally, God again emphasizes His everlasting nature saying, "This is my name forever, and thus I am to be remembered throughout all generations" (Exodus 3:15, ESV). Naming Himself personally to Moses, God highlights both His eternal nature and His relational nature. He emphasizes His presence. The name *YHWH* is connected to all these things.

Lord = Adonai, God as Master

Additionally, God is holy and set apart. His power is to be recognized and submitted to. This is captured in the word *Adonai* or *Lord.*

Read Exodus 4:10 and 4:13. What is Moses talking to God about in these verses?

How is God's name rendered when Moses directly addresses God in verse 10 and 13?

In both verses when Moses speaks to God, *Lord* has lowercase letters, representing the Hebrew *Adonai.* This word is used only of God, and it appears in contexts where God is addressed with reverence and submission.[4] Moses cautiously begs God to send someone else to Pharoah in Exodus 4, doubtless aware of the possible impertinence of his request. Thus, He addresses God as *Adonai,* acknowledging the mastery and rule of God.

Side By Side

When *Adonai* and *YHWH* appear next to one another, as they do in Isaiah 30:15, you will not see "Lord LORD." Most translations use either "the Lord GOD" (ESV, CSB, KJV, and others) or "the Sovereign Lord" (NIV, NLT, and others).

Putting these two different names side by side combines two aspects of God, but it might not be obvious at first glance. It is worth your time to understand the distinctions your translation makes in how it renders the different names of God.

Holy, Holy, Holy

Back to God's name in Isaiah 30:15, specifically the part following the comma. In English it is consistently expressed "the Holy One of Israel," a translation of the Hebrew *Qedosh Yisrael. Qedosh* means "holy" or "set apart." Scholars say this word emphasizes God's separation from and aversion to sin.[5] *Yisrael* means "of Israel." Together these words create the title "the Holy One of Israel." God's holiness makes Him completely other and separate from humans, but He is also the God of Israel and therefore relational.

Why So Many Names?

Putting all that detail together, we see the invitation offered in Isaiah 30:15 comes from the "Lord GOD, the Holy One of Israel." This is an even richer picture of God's nature. This juxtaposition of God's names occurs just this one time in Scripture. This unique combination of God's names doubly emphasizes two seemingly opposite ideas into one description of our amazing God.

---

[4] "H136 - 'ăḏōnāy - Gesenius' Hebrew-Chaldee Lexicon." *Blue Letter Bible,* www.blueletterbible.org/lexicon/h136/esv/wlc/0-1/. Accessed 21 May 2024.

[5] "H6918 - Qāḏôš - Strong's Hebrew Lexicon (KJV)." *Blue Letter Bible,* www.blueletterbible.org/lexicon/h6918/kjv/wlc/0-1/.

God is transcendent: Holy and set apart, mysterious and outside the full grasp of human experience or understanding. God is immanent: Near, personal, relational, ever reaching toward us. Together the "Lord God, the Holy One of Israel" offers a window into the expansive nature of God. He is holy, masterful, and powerful; therefore, He is **able** to save. He is near, personal, and relational; therefore, He is **willing** to save.

This Isaiah 30:15 naming of God expresses the rich fullness of His nature. This is who invites you to return and rest in Him. This personal and powerful God invites you to intimacy.

Lesson Three: Spotlight on Salvation

O loving God, Jesus, Holy Spirit, come into my time of study today. Give me eyes to see and ears to hear what you desire to show me in your Word.

More on This Invitation

In the early 18th century, British pastor Matthew Henry wrote a commentary on the Bible. There he poses a question still relevant today, even if his language is a little archaic: "Would we be saved from the evil of every calamity, guarded against the temptation of it, and secured from the curse of it?"[6]

My answer is a resounding, "Yes!" How about you? Look back at the "hard-pressed" places you identified in Chapter One. Then fill in the phrases below.

I want to be saved from . . .

I would like to be guarded against the temptation of . . .

I want to be secure in . . .

Henry gives us the solution to salvation and security, drawn from Isaiah 30:15: "It must be in returning and in rest."

We absolutely want to be saved, protected, and secured from harm. Contemporary culture is built around this. From self-help books to preventative health care to every labor-saving device you can think of, we swim in a sea of options for salvation of some sort. Not all offers of salvation are created equally, however. In Isaiah 30, we see that Judah looking to Egypt for salvation from Assyria was a bad plan, an alliance "not of God's Spirit."

True rescue and salvation can only come from God and at His direction. In Isaiah 30:15, God offers a pathway to salvation from Assyria and their threats to Jerusalem. It is through returning to Him and resting in Him. The *Ancient Hebrew Lexicon* reveals this beautiful picture of the Hebrew word for salvation used in Isaiah 30:15: "when one of the flock is in

---

[6] Henry, Matthew. "Isaiah 30 - Henry's Complete Commentary on the Bible." *StudyLight.org*, www.studylight.org/commentaries/eng/mhm/isaiah-30.html.

trouble the shepherd rescues it."[7] That sounds a lot like something Jesus mentioned in a parable in Luke 15:4-5. "What man of you, having a hundred sheep, if he has lost one of them, does not leave the ninety-nine in the open country, and go after the one that is lost until he finds it? And when he has found it, he lays it on his shoulder, rejoicing" (ESV).

Repent, Return, Come Home

The invitation to salvation comes through both returning to Him and resting in Him. The word *returning* is also expressed as *repenting* in some translations of Isaiah 30:15.

Read Deuteronomy 30:1-3. What action is included with returning to Him in verse 2?

What is the result according to verse 3?

Read Jeremiah 3:22. What will God do when we return to Him?

Read Hosea 6:1-3. What phrases come after "let us" in verses 1 and 3?

According to Hosea 6:2, what ultimate purpose does God have for us?

These verses reveal that God is responsive to our return to Him. He will have compassion on us, heal us, come to us faithfully, and He is waiting to be known intimately. Hosea 6:2 even connects the invitation to return to the Lord with a prophetic picture of Jesus' resurrection.

The Hebrew word translated "returning" or "repentance" in Isaiah 30:15 reveals two other beautiful pictures. The word is *shuba*, a noun form used just this once in the Bible. (Its root word *sub*, which we studied the first lesson of this chapter, is used more than a thousand

---

[7] "Strong's #3467 - Old Testament Hebrew Lexical Dictionary." *StudyLight.org*, www.studylight.org/lexicons/eng/hebrew/3467.html.

times.) *Shuba* can also mean "retirement or withdrawal, as from war," according to *Brown-Driver-Briggs Lexicon*.[8] The *Ancient Hebrew Lexicon* identifies it as "a returning to one's place of residence."[9]

Have you ever thought of coming to the Lord as coming home after engaging in battle? Or as coming back to the place you live? What a restful, comforting image. Our day-to-day lives can feel like we are soldiers in a battle-filled land. We can come home to God.

Oh, Sweet Rest

Hosea 6:3b paints this picture: ". . . he will come to us as the showers, as the spring rains water the earth" (ESV). One of the most restful things I know is sitting on a porch listening to the sound of a steady, heavy spring rain, with its cool dampness and soothing rhythms. Several times the Lord has used just such a setting to deeply quiet my soul. He comes to us with this restfulness on offer, and, just like the rain, He comes to us again and again.

Matthew 11:28-30 is a famous invitation from Jesus, which describes both Him and what an intimate relationship with Him looks like. The rendition found in Eugene Peterson's paraphrase in *The Message* says this:

> Are you tired? Worn out? Burned out on religion? Come to me. Get away with me and you'll recover your life. I'll show you how to take a real rest. Walk with me and work with me—watch how I do it. Learn the unforced rhythms of grace. I won't lay anything heavy or ill-fitting on you. Keep company with me and you'll learn to live freely and lightly.

How does Jesus describe the people He is inviting?

What does He offer?

How does He say we can receive this rest?

---

[8] Brown-Driver-Briggs. "H7729 - Šûḇâ - Strong's Hebrew Lexicon (KJV)." *Blue Letter Bible*, www.blueletterbible.org/lexicon/h7729/kjv/wlc/0-1/.

[9] "Strong's #7729 - Old Testament Hebrew Lexical Dictionary." *StudyLight.org*, www.studylight.org/lexicons/eng/hebrew/7729.html.

What is the result of this rest?

This is step-by-step companionship and side-by-side intimacy. In that position, we can learn to live with ease and lightness from Him.

As you finish this lesson, go back to your earlier answers in response to Matthew Henry's quote. Read through them again, thinking of them in light of God's invitation to return and to rest. Let that invitation wash over you. Write a prayer of response to God below.

Lesson Four: Spotlight on Strength

O loving God, Jesus, Holy Spirit, come into my time of study today. Give me eyes to see and ears to hear what you desire to show me in your Word.

Even More on This Invitation

Today, we begin again with Matthew Henry. He poses a second question in his commentary on Isaiah 30:15: "Would we be strengthened to do what is required of us and to bear what is laid upon us?"[10]

Again, I suspect our answer is a strong, "Yes!" Personalize his question below.

I would like strength to face the requirements to . . .

I want strength to bear . . .

Henry's commentary again points us to the solution. "It must be in quietness and confidence," he writes, referencing God's invitation in Isaiah 30:15.

One reason for Judah's ongoing attraction to lesser gods like Egypt might be because they offered "the path of least resistance." Let's be honest, we aren't very different. It is easy to feel we are running on empty at times. We are busy and burdened, living in a complex, fast-paced world. Very few people have a margin for anything but the quickest and least difficult option to solve a problem. Wouldn't it be great to have an unlimited source of strength to propel us through all the twists and turns of our lives?

Fuel For Strength

As any athlete will tell you, fueling your body is important. Failure to fuel adequately can result in something endurance athletes call "hitting the wall." It is as sudden and unpleasant as it sounds. Proper calories and hydration keep the paralysis of that depletion at bay. The same is true spiritually. We must be well-fueled spiritually or we too can become exhausted and immobile, like athletes hitting the proverbial wall.

---

[10] Henry, Matthew. "Isaiah 30 - Henry's Complete Commentary on the Bible." *StudyLight.org*, www.studylight.org/commentaries/eng/mhm/isaiah-30.html.

Read Isaiah 55:1-3. Who is God inviting?

What is the invitation?

The metaphor of this invitation equates eating with listening to God (verse 2), finding satisfaction and delight in something we cannot purchase through our own labor.
Read John 7:37-38. Who is speaking and what is the offer?

How is this invitation similar to Isaiah 55:1-3?

What is the requirement to receive the living waters of John 7:37-38?

Read John 7:39. Who is identified as the "rivers" Jesus says will flow from the hearts of those who believe in Him?

What Sort of Fuel?

Jesus told His disciples that when He returned to Heaven after His resurrection, He would send the Holy Spirit to them (John 14:16-17). Through this Spirit, He said, they would receive power (Acts 1:8). Believers in Christ have the very Spirit of God living inside them, according to Romans 8:9-11. The Holy Spirit is supernatural fuel for spiritual strength. Let's learn more about the power He brings into the life of a believer.
Read John 14:26. What is the mission and ministry of the Holy Spirit?

Read John 16:8. What does this reveal about the mission and ministry of the Spirit?

Read John 16:13. What will the Spirit do?

Read John 16:14-15. How is the Spirit related to Jesus and to God the Father?

John 16:13-15 reveals the Trinity. The Spirit's declaration of truth flows freely between the union of Father, Son, and Holy Spirit. These verses describe the unity and intimacy within the Trinity.

Read John 15:4-5. What do these verses say about one who is **not** united to Christ?

Write a summary of what you have learned about the type of fuel the Holy Spirit offers.

Go back to Isaiah 30:15 and read the invitation once more. What does it say "shall be [our] strength?"

Some translations use the phrases "in silence and hope" or "quiet confidence" or "quietness and trust." They all paint a picture of tranquility and of clinging to something or someone for security, safety, or strength. God is inviting us to rest and relationship based in deep trust and confidence in God, who dwells in believers in Christ through the Holy Spirit.

Invitation to Relationship

When we are fed and nourished by an intimate relationship with God through the Holy Spirit within us, we can have confidence that we will be guided into all truth and convicted with respect to sin and righteousness (John 16:8-10). This is the food that gives great strength. This is the intimacy that leads to rest. Another passage combines quietness, strength, and salvation like Isaiah 30:15 does.

Read Exodus 14:13-14. What does it say about what you are to do in a battle?

We will close this lesson like we did the last one. Look back at your list of desires for strength from the beginning of this lesson. Think of these desires through the lens of Holy Spirit fuel and the strength of God fighting for you. Write a prayer of response below.

Lesson Five: The Invitation With a Road Map

O loving God, Jesus, Holy Spirit, come into my time of study today. Give me eyes to see and ears to hear what you desire to show me in your Word.

Review the Road Map

The Isaiah 30:15 invitation offers us a "road map" of four words leading us to the benefits of salvation and strength. Can you recall and write them below without looking up the verse?

Your Bible translation may have synonyms for the four words found in the ESV: *returning, rest, quietness,* and *trust.* Whatever the exact wording, the verse forms a map whose path runs straight to the heart of a loving and powerful God. It echoes many other invitations of Scripture, none more important than this one from Jesus: ". . . I am the way, and the truth, and the life. No one comes to the Father except through me" John 14:6 (ESV).

Jesus is the way to the Father. The Father, according to Isaiah 30:15, longs for us to return and rest in Him, to find strength through quietness and trust in Him.

This invitation to salvation from enemies and the strength to withstand attacks should have been very attractive to the original recipients of Isaiah's prophecy. Sadly, however, their initial response wasn't favorable. They didn't accept the invitation.

Choices and Consequences

In the last chapter, we explored two different responses to hard circumstances. God's children had the choice to run to other sources for help or to rest in Him. We have the same choice.

We haven't spent time with the remaining portion of Isaiah 30:15. In the ESV translation, four sad words end this verse: "But you were unwilling." The original audience for this invitation was unwilling to return, rest, and quietly trust God.

Read Isaiah 30:9-10. What else were God's children unwilling to do?

What did they want instead of truth?

Read Isaiah 30:16-17. What choice did God's children make?

What was the result according to verse 17?

Based on what we have studied so far, why might the people living in Jerusalem have responded the way they did to their circumstances?

What similarities do you see between your own responses to God and the responses to God of Isaiah's original audience?

I have more in common with the ancient residents of Jerusalem than I might want to admit. I am not immune from temptation to alliances with lesser gods and powerless providers. Is this true of you? Maybe we find ourselves so worn down from trying to juggle all our things that we cannot imagine slowing down, stopping, or surrendering to Him.

Maybe we think we can handle things ourselves. Our culture regularly teaches us we don't need strength from outside sources. Voices around us cheer us on to "live our own truth" or to "show up for ourselves" by "putting ourselves first." This advice is about as worthless as God says the Egyptians are in Isaiah 30:7.

Those relentless voices set us up for a difficult time. They suggest that we are in danger if we admit our vulnerability and our need for a Savior and His strength. Yet, vulnerability and honesty are two key ingredients to any relationship. As I write this, I am praying for you. I am asking God to give you a soft heart to consider what I am about to ask you to do.

Consider the Invitation Anew

Ask the Holy Spirit to guide you to examine with honesty your own response to the Isaiah 30:15 invitation to intimacy. Are you inclined to run right now or to rest? Do you want "smooth things" rather than the instruction of the Lord? Do you fighting and flail against your circumstances, trying to tread water in your own strength? Or are you ready to lie back and rest in Jesus, holding His hand while you float above all the churning waves in quietness and trust?

Wherever you are in response to God's invitation to more intimacy, even if it is a place of fear or of skepticism, hold on to these words from Romans 5:1: "Therefore, since we have been made right in God's sight by faith, we have peace with God because of what Jesus Christ our Lord has done for us" (NLT).

Chapter Two Prayer and Promise

We have taken a deep dive into one verse from Isaiah 30:15. We discovered more about our great God through studying His unique name. We found God is transcendent: powerful, mighty, mysterious, and "other." We also learned that He is simultaneously immanent: near, relational, inviting and "with us." He is both mighty to save and tender to bend close to us.

He extends a wondrous invitation, much needed amid our busy, demanding, and sometimes confusing lives. God offers us salvation from things that threaten us, and He offers us strength through the Holy Spirit to face hard things that seem too much to bear.

We have examined the path of returning, rest, quietness, and trust in this lesson. As pastor David Guzik writes in commentary on Isaiah 30:15, these four characteristics taken together provide fuel for "a real trust in God's promise." He notes, "There is no person walking this earth more powerful than a child of God boldly and properly trusting the promise of the living God."[11]

You can respond to an invitation to an intimate relationship with a powerful, personal God.

Key Practice: Look over your responses to previous reflection questions on Chapter One, Lesson Five and Chapter Two, Lessons Three and Four. Do you sense God fighting for you? Where do you need more saving, more strengthening? Use your answers as a basis for a prayer of responding to God's invitation to you.

Key Promise: "My flesh and my heart may fail, but God is the strength of my heart and my portion forever."

Psalm 73:26 (ESV)

Heavenly Father, thank you for loving your children so much that you speak truth to us. Thank you for extending an invitation to return to you and find salvation and strength. Would you give me strength to accept it through your powerful Holy Spirit within me? I long to experience the rest and confidence described in your Word. May it be so in the name of Jesus.

---

[11] Guzik, David. "Study Guide for Isaiah 30." *Blue Letter Bible*, www.blueletterbible.org/comm/guzik_david/study-guide/isaiah/isaiah-30.cfm?a=709018.

Notes

Chapter Three: Recover Your Identity

Key Idea: You can recover and walk in your identity as a beloved child of God.

Key Verse: "See what kind of love the Father has given to us, that we should be called children of God; and so we are." 1 John 3:1 (ESV)

Even amid chastising His children for turning away from Him, God extends a path back to His peace, rest, and provision. We are often like these wayward children, turning to resources other than God to meet our needs. Isn't He gracious and good to continually call us back to Him?

The Isaiah 30:15 invitation is extended to those God calls His children. In the Old Testament, that designation usually refers to the nation of Israel. However, throughout God's story in the Bible, we see His heart for all nations. (See Genesis 12:1-3, Psalm 22:27-28, Isaiah 25:6-8, and Daniel 7:14, among others). The New Testament reveals that the invitation to become a child of God has been fully extended to all who will receive Christ Jesus as Lord.

When someone believes in Jesus' saving work on the cross and in His resurrection and ascension, they have accepted the initial call to salvation extended through the gospel of Christ. Accepting that invitation allows a person to receive a new identity: that of God's beloved child (John 1:12).

After accepting God's invitation to salvation, however, we must respond to His continual invitation to intimacy, to return, and to rest. This invitation to experience more of Him is true for a new Christian or one who has walked with Him for decades. Accepting His ongoing invitation to rest in Him both forms and strengthens our identity.

Our identity is important. Confusion about it can derail our intimacy with the Father, His Son, and the Spirit within us. In this chapter's lessons we will explore how we identify ourselves and what it means to be a child of God.

Lesson One: Your Identity is Important

O loving God, Jesus, Holy Spirit, come into my time of study today. Give me eyes to see and ears to hear what you desire to show me in your Word.

Too Many Hats

To assess how to create more margin in my life several years ago, I made a list of the various roles and relationships I had at the time. I was stunned to discover I was trying to juggle more than twenty roles in more than ten different arenas. My identities included wife, mom, home school educator, prayer partner, Sunday school teacher, tennis coach, caregiver to aging parents, and numerous others.

To my horror, I realized one item that did not appear on my list of identities: child of God. In the busyness of all those things, I had lost sight of the key relationship which holds my key identity.

That got my attention. It gave a clear, ugly picture of where I was oriented: toward performing, people pleasing, and pride. It showed me where I wasn't oriented: toward God.

Women are especially susceptible to this. We wear a lot of hats. This not only scatters our energy but opens us to the attacks of the enemy of our souls. Satan desires intently to separate us from our identity in Christ. He knows it will make us fearful, worn down, and leave us doubting God's goodness.

Start today with the same assessment. Make a list of the names of people or groups with whom you have key relationships. For each one, list the role or roles you play.

Person or group	Role or roles I play

Stubborn Children

Isaiah 30 opens with God announcing who He is speaking to: His children. While the descriptions vary by translation ("stubborn," "rebellious," or "obstinate"), the audience doesn't change. God is a Father addressing His wayward sons and daughters. He is speaking truth. Though it may not sound so to our modern ears, He is speaking truth in love.

According to the *Brown-Driver-Briggs Hebrew Lexicon*, the Hebrew word for *children* in Isaiah 30:1 expresses "intimate and gracious relation to God."[12] God is pursuing His beloved children. He calls them to a place of safety in Him and away from a route of pain with the Egyptians. This is bold, intimate, fatherly love, filled with care. It reminds me of Proverbs 3:12: "For the LORD corrects those he loves, just as a father corrects a child in whom he delights" (NLT).

What does Proverbs 3:12 reveal about the relationship between love and correction?

We Are Children Too

In the Old Testament, the Israelites are described as God's children. The picture of God as father is clear in texts like Deuteronomy 14:1-2, Isaiah 63:16, and Isaiah 64:8. God's covenant relationship with Israel included a commitment to them analogous to a father's commitment to his children. Jesus spoke of God as His father often. After Christ's resurrection, New Testament writings indicate an expansion of the family of God. The New Testament teaches that those redeemed by Christ and led by the Spirit are "children of God."

Read Galatians 3:26-29. What does verse 26 say qualifies one to be a child of God?

How are Christ followers related to Abraham according to verse 29?

Faith in Jesus is how a person becomes a child of God. Galatians says belonging to Christ makes us Abraham's offspring as well, right alongside those children being addressed in Isaiah 30. Thus, we can read Isaiah 30 as a text addressed to us today. We, too, are His children, also tempted to look elsewhere rather than to God for help or for our identity.

Read Romans 8:14-16. According to verse 14, what qualifies one to be a child of God?

---

12 Brown-Driver-Briggs. "H1121 - Bēn - Strong's Hebrew Lexicon (KJV)." *Blue Letter Bible*, www.blueletterbible.org/lexicon/h1121/kjv/wlc/0-1/.

What does the word *Abba* in verse 15 mean?

What does verse 16 say about how to be confident of being God's child?

According to Romans, one who is led by the Spirit of God is a child of God. If that is you, you can cry "Abba" or "Daddy" to God! This identity as His child frees you from fear and adopts you into His family. When you have this adoption, you can be confident of it at the deepest level, because the Spirit of God in you assures you of your identity as God's child.

Read John 1:12-13. What do you learn about how to become a child of God?

Read John 3:3-7. What is the relationship between this and John 1:13?

These two sections of John paint a picture of becoming God's children through faith. This faith enables a new birth into the kingdom of God—a spiritual rebirth, bringing new life to all who will receive. Part of that new life includes a new identity: if you are in Christ, you are a daughter of the Most High God. That makes you a princess.

A difficult fact of living in a broken world is that many people have fractured relationships with their earthly parents. This can deeply color and shape one's thinking about what God as a father even means. If this is true for you, know that your loving God sees you and loves you deeply. He does this even if you cannot yet find yourself embracing His fatherhood in a comforting or meaningful way. I pray He will meet you with His deep, loving care in a special way as we continue exploring the wonderful identity we have as His daughters.

Lesson Two: Where Are Our Hearts Aligned?

O loving God, Jesus, Holy Spirit, come into my time of study today. Give me eyes to see and ears to hear what you desire to show me in your Word.

Disconnected Identity

In the last lesson, I shared a realization I made once concerning where I found my identity—externally in a lot of different roles and responsibilities. I knew and loved Christ, but the many roles I was resting in had eclipsed my professed identity as a Christ follower. As Luke 6:44 reminds, "each tree is known by its own fruit" (ESV). Looking at the fruit I was producing, I saw I wasn't following Christ as much as following the path of the next item on my to-do list. My identity was centered more in what I did than in who I was resting in. External actions revealed my inside—my heart—wasn't exactly where I thought it was. There was a disconnect.

Professed Identity Versus Lived Identity

The ancient children of God had a similar issue. Throughout the Bible, the people of Israel often pridefully asserted their identity as descendants of Abraham and as God's chosen people. But an external identity is not the same as living in a God-centered identity.

John the Baptist warned about this very thing when he preached to Jewish leaders at the time of Christ. "Don't just say to each other, 'We're safe, for we are descendants of Abraham.' That means nothing . . . Yes, every tree that does not produce good fruit will be chopped down and thrown into the fire" (Matthew 3:9-10 NLT). Notice the imagery of a tree being known by its fruit again. Isaiah 30 reveals the fruit of the lives of God's children in Isaiah's days.

Read Isaiah 30:6. What does this show Judah was willing to do for help?

What does that reveal about their hearts?

Read Isaiah 30:9-11. How is Judah's relationship to God described here?

What does that reveal about their hearts?

Read Isaiah 30:16-17. What actions are described in these verses?

What do these actions reveal about Judah?

In the first half of Isaiah 30, God's children are not living from a place of confidence in Him. They may have outwardly identified as God's chosen people, but inwardly they didn't trust in His power to care for them. Motivated by fear, they sought help but not from God, preferring to hear of ease and illusions of safety. Ironically, they chose a hard path "through a land of trouble and anguish" (Isaiah 30:6 ESV). As we saw in Lesson One, they would rather run away than rest in Him (Isaiah 30:16).

Disconnected Heart

Spiritual hypocrisy is nothing new. It is seen across history and is often recorded in the Bible. It also hasn't disappeared in our day.

Read Isaiah 29:13. According to this verse, where are the hearts of God's people?

Centuries later, Jesus quoted this verse to Pharisees critiquing Him for failing to follow Jewish cultural practices of handwashing before eating.

Read Mark 7:1-15. Where did the Pharisees gain their identity?

What does this reveal about their hearts toward God?

Read Matthew 23:25-28. What is Jesus accusing the Pharisees of?

What does he say in verse 26 will solve their hypocrisy?

What is not aligned for them, according to Jesus?

Read Luke 6:43-45. What is the relationship between our hearts and our actions?

The truth of our identity eventually flows from the inner man to the outer man. There is a saying, "Fake it 'til you make it." This is not something the Bible affirms. Identity comes from inside to outside, not the other way around.

Read Luke 12:1-3. What does this teach about hypocrisy and identity?

We see in these passages the potential for a strong disconnect between hearts and actions. We also learn the heart will ultimately be revealed, regardless of what things might look like on the outside. Jesus had something else to say to the Pharisees about these matters: "You like to appear righteous in public, but God knows your hearts. What this world honors is detestable in the sight of God" (Luke 16:15 NLT).

What is important to God is the heart, not appearances (1 Samuel 16:7). Your heart and your true identity are deeply related.

Forms Without Power

Jesus essentially told the Pharisees their external behavior was a veneer, a false front. Paul warned Timothy to stay away from people who had such a veneer. He described these people as "having the appearance of godliness, but denying its power" (2 Timothy 3:5 ESV).

In more contemporary language, Eugene Peterson calls them people who "make a show of religion" (MSG). A "show of religion" has no power—relationship with God has power.

Where do you see "a form of godliness without power" in the culture around you?

Do you see this at all in your own life? If so, how?

If you depend on only external forms of religion to see you through, you will discover that it isn't of much value. The children of God in Judah thought they needed to run to Egypt for help instead of God, and no wonder. They didn't really know their identity as His children at the heart level.

God critiqued His people for what is essentially shallow faith. They didn't know Him; they just knew some stuff about Him. That isn't the power that is needed for day-to-day life, especially when the Assyrians are knocking at the door. There's a difference between adherence to a religion and acceptance of a relationship.

Close now with some heart examination. Look back at the list of identities you made on page 44. Take into consideration the truths we've studied in this lesson. Spend some time in prayer with the Lord about your heart.

Lesson Three: Children of God Have a Bounty of Blessings

O loving God, Jesus, Holy Spirit, come into my time of study today. Give me eyes to see and ears to hear what you desire to show me in your Word.

Not By Your Own Doing

After studying passages like Matthew 23, Luke 6, and others in the last lesson, you might be tempted to self-critique or self-management. You might be thinking, "I had better get busy working to get my heart right." This is not what the good news of Jesus offers. The work isn't solely up to you. In Christ, we are changed by the power of the Holy Spirit.

Read 2 Corinthians 3:16-18. How does our transformation come about?

These verses describe a transformation by degrees. It is a process. Theologians describe that process as sanctification. It is something that takes time, and 2 Corinthians 3:18 reveals that it is guided and accomplished by the Holy Spirit.

We cannot change ourselves in our own strength any more than Judah could rely on Egypt to fix their problems with the Assyrians. We can only cooperate with the work of God within us. As our invitation in Isaiah 30:15 reminds us, it is only by resting in God that we find salvation and strength. That is the secret of embracing our identity in Christ.

Sometimes we get impatient with ourselves, feeling we can never measure up. Our actions don't match our words, and we get discouraged. We will talk more about this in future lessons. Today, discover some of the wonder your identity in Christ holds.

What Does a Princess Wear?

Read Isaiah 61:10. What garments and clothes are described here?

It only makes sense that a child of God, a princess, would get to wear a royal robe of righteousness! The Bible describes more clothes for the child of God. Galatians 3:27 tells us: "For all of you who were baptized into Christ have clothed yourselves with Christ" (NIV).

A child of God wears the new clothes of Christ. As you embrace your identity as God's beloved daughter, you get to wear Jesus. As your heart is transformed, your actions are too. Your insides and your outsides line up to the praise and glory of God (Matthew 5:16).

Royalty Lives in Richness

As God's daughter, you belong to the most royal household in all of space and time. There is not a higher King than the Lord GOD, the Holy One of Israel. Certain privileges and powers are available to members of a royal family simply by virtue of having been born with that identity.

Earlier in this chapter, we encountered this truth in Galatians 3:26: "For you are all children of God through faith in Christ Jesus" (NLT).

There is a tiny Greek word here connecting us with Christ's tremendous power. The word is *en*—a two-letter preposition often translated "in" or "through" in English. It appears in the phrase *en Christos* or "in Christ" in Galatians 3:26.

According to *Thayer's Greek Lexicon*, the phrase *en Christos* describes being united with or wholly joined to Jesus. New Testament writer Paul used this phrase (and its synonyms) frequently to indicate we can be "ingrafted as it were in Christ, in fellowship and union with Christ."[13] By faith in Christ, we are not only children of God, but we are united with Jesus.

This phrase opens a world of gifts and truths we need to take into our identity. We will look at just a small sample of them here. For each reference below, write down what is available to you "in Christ."

Romans 6:11

Romans 6:23

Romans 8:1

Romans 8:38-39

Galatians 3:14

Ephesians 1:3-8

---

[13] "Strong's #1722 - Ἐν - Thayer's Expanded Definition." *StudyLight.org*, www.studylight.org/lexicons/eng/greek/1722.html.

Ephesians 2:10

1 Timothy 1:13-14

2 Timothy 2:1

That is a list full of privilege and power, which should help you begin to see the abundance that is yours as God's child. There are many more passages declaring the identity we have in Christ. As 1 Corinthians 2:9 proclaims: "That is what the Scriptures mean when they say, 'No eye has seen, no ear has heard, and no mind has imagined what God has prepared for those who love him'" (NLT).

Lesson Four: Don't Live Like an Orphan

O loving God, Jesus, Holy Spirit, come into my time of study today. Give me eyes to see and ears to hear what you desire to show me in your Word.

Riches Under Attack

As God's daughter, you have access to many privileges. But you live in a broken, fallen world; a world at war. At both the supernatural level and in the natural realm, you face opposition to embracing your full identity in Christ and all it brings. 1 Peter 5:8 reminds, "Be sober-minded, be alert. Your adversary the devil is prowling around like a roaring lion, looking for anyone he can devour" (CSB).

You have an enemy. He wants to bully you into doubting the truth of who you are. One of the ways he does this is by trying to make you believe you are an orphan instead of a beloved child.

A Lament for Loss of Fatherhood

During Old Testament times, God's children were often in circumstances that caused them to despair. At times they even doubted whether God was with them at all. We explored some of these in Chapter One.

Lamentations is thought to have been written soon after the Babylonians destroyed Jerusalem and its temple in 586 BC. The book looks back at this destruction with grief. Lamentations 5:3 declares: "We have become orphans, fatherless; our mothers are widows" (CSB). Lamentations 5 goes on to catalog a list of circumstances that led the author to draw such a conclusion.

Skim through Lamentations 5, taking note of any orphan circumstances you find.

The circumstances described in Lamentations occurred nearly 200 years later than those we've studied in Isaiah 30. Our Chapter One study revealed Judah turning away from God. While King Hezekiah's repentance brought a reprieve from the Assyrians, peace was not lasting. Later a string of idolatrous and evil kings ultimately led to Judah's fall to Babylon. As Judah forgot, ignored, or fully rejected God over time, they lived more and more like orphans. The consequences were disastrous.

Similarly, our ever-changing circumstances can war against us embracing our true identity. If we look only at our circumstances to get our bearings, we also may feel we are orphans. We must remember to look beyond our circumstances.

Read Hebrews 12:1-2. Where are you to fix your eyes?

This passage speaks of encouragement, endurance, and the example of Jesus. Even more, it points to Christ's enduring the cross and ascending victoriously over sin and death, finally being seated at the right hand of the throne of God.

He did all that for you.

Be Alert!

An "orphan spirit" describes a reality that is sadly all too true for some Christians who live as though their identity in Christ isn't real. They live as though abandoned by God, rejected, forgotten, or overlooked. That point of view wars significantly against embracing identity in Christ. We have explored some of the riches of this identity. Now, take time to pay attention to how your heart aligns with the truth of your identity in Christ.

The chart on this page and the next one outlines a comparison of experiences based on the truths you've studied containing the phrase *en Christos*.

The left-hand column shows some characteristics of "orphan living," though this is not a comprehensive list. In the middle column are the verses from the last lesson. The column on the right summarizes the characteristics derived from those verses. These are characteristics of one living in the identity of a child of God.

Meditate on these lists. Ask the Holy Spirit to help you identify places where you might be living more out of an orphan mentality than out of your identity as a beloved daughter.

Orphan experiences	Verse	Daughter experiences
- Feels powerless or helpless in the face of temptation - Has a victim mentality - Feels beaten down or in "survival mode"	Romans 6:11	- Empowered in face of temptation - Victorious in Christ - Vibrant and life-filled
- Fearful of the future - Doubtful and suspicion-filled	Romans 6:23	- Believes her future is wonderful - Hope-filled
- Critical of self and others - Little to no sense of freedom - Restless, insecure, lack of peace	Romans 8:1	- Lives without condemnation - Experiences Freedom - Is restful and peaceful

- Unsure of God's love - Often feels isolated or alone - Unable to sense God's presence - Fearful of death - Fearful of present or future circumstances - Hyper-vigilant about possible threats or danger	Romans 8:38-39	- Confident of God's love and protection - Experiences God's presence - Feels loved and assured
- Insecure about her standing with God and His family - Feels excluded or an outsider - Unsure of blessing or acceptance by God, therefore, relies on her works to "earn" her place in His family - Lives by "sight," therefore uses circumstances to determine her status with God	Galatians 3:14	- Knows she is included in God's family - Knows she is blessed by God - Lives in step with and is empowered by God's Spirit - Assured by the Spirit that she belongs - Lives by faith; confident of her status with God because of the Spirit
- Has a scarcity mindset - Doesn't feel beloved or delighted in by God - Self-critical - Weighed down by guilt - Doubts God's grace to her - Judgmental and ungracious to herself and others	Ephesians 1:3-8	- Has an abundance mindset - Knows she is chosen by God, adopted, and delighted in - Believes she is blameless in God's sight - Experiences God's grace and kindness -Knows she is freely forgiven
- Unsure of having purpose - Feels competitive with others - Searching for ways to find meaning or significance	Ephesians 2:10	- Knows God has plans and purposes specifically for her - Follows God's lead in how to live and serve
- Experiences shame about the past; isn't sure she is forgiven - Struggles to accept grace	1 Timothy 1:13-14	- Is not ashamed of her past - Lives in grace, faith, and love in the present
- Feels weak and timid - Doubts she will have strength for challenges	2 Timothy 2:1	- Experiences strength that comes through grace

Scan here to get a single page version of this chart for your personal use.

Lesson Five: The Call to Surrender

O loving God, Jesus, Holy Spirit, come into my time of study today. Give me eyes to see and ears to hear what you desire to show me in your Word.

What Kind of Princess Are You?

Women are surrounded by princesses from a very young age. The one who captured my heart was Diana of Themyscira, otherwise known as Wonder Woman. You might be picturing Gal Gadot, but I am a child of the 1970s. It was all Lynda Carter for me. I still remember standing in my yard as a ten-year-old, spinning around and hoping for the heroine transformation to happen. She was a hoped-for identity, an inspiration, and muse.

Even as an adult she held sway over me. I collected all the things: Wonder Woman lunch boxes, magnets, cups, stationery, you name it. For years, I slept in a pair of Wonder Woman boxer shorts, taking them in my suitcase on every trip. (Are you seeing the way I was literally clothing myself in the wrong identity?)

For a long time, Wonder Woman was the princess for me, until one September day in 2014 at a ladies' retreat. On a rainy Saturday afternoon on a balcony overlooking the stormy Gulf of Mexico, God told me He wanted to deliver me from Wonder Woman.

In a teary conversation, we talked through my weariness, worries, and wounds. He gently showed me when I tried to be Wonder Woman, I exhausted myself. But I didn't want to let her go. She was a strong, capable, truth-seeking rescuer, who was humble and unexpected. I loved those things so much. I wanted to be those things for God so much because I thought that was what would please Him.

The Holy Spirit showed me the things I loved about Wonder Woman are also true of Jesus. While she is a cartoon, He is real. When I ran around trying to be Wonder Woman, even if my motives were to please God, I had it all backwards. God is the rescuer, not me. I am the one who is rescued. I had been living out of my own resources, trying to rescue myself and anyone else who would let me. I thought that was how to serve and please God. It was utterly wearing me out.

Is it Time for a Breakup?

God told me it was time to break up with Wonder Woman. So, I did. I prayed earnestly, inviting His presence and forgiveness into that messy, muddled place. I surrendered trying to be the rescuer instead of the rescued. I knew very little of what it would look like, but I knew I had to do it.

That afternoon, I took my Wonder Woman boxer shorts out of my suitcase and quietly deposited them into the trash bins below the beach house. Then I shared with others what God had asked me to do, because I knew I needed accountability. It was the beginning of a beautiful transformation for me.

Looking back, I now realize that I was longing to wear an identity I can find wholly and completely in Him. I just had the power source all mixed up. I thought I had to be a Wonder Woman of service and perfection to please God and "earn" my place in His family. I began discovering He was my strength instead.

Roadblocks and Wrestling

You've seen some of the wrong identities I have worn. Read between the lines of my story and you'll see the orphan mindset I have battled. These things still pop up from time to time. 2 Corinthians 3:18 promises we are being transformed from one degree of glory to another. Transformation takes time, but God draws me ever more toward Him.

One of the most telling features of orphan living is what I discovered during my Wonder Woman break up: As God's children we don't have to perform to get love, and we don't have to "earn our keep" to get security.

When you encounter the transforming grace of Jesus Christ, there is a path that leads away from orphan thinking in all its many ugly varieties. God can help you recover your identity as God's beloved.

No Hiding

Honesty before our Heavenly Father is essential to intimacy with Him. Some people find being honest with God is difficult. They are fearful of rejection or of the pain of coming face to face with their own junk.

Read Psalm 139:1-12. What does this reveal about trying to hide from God?

How do you feel about this sort of intimacy? Is it more thrilling or terrifying to you?

Honesty with God is important. Sometimes it is very, very hard. I trembled as I admitted to God in 2014 how much I had pursued the ideal of a fictional character instead of Jesus. But He already knew that, and He met me with grace. Just as earthly parents love their children no matter what (at times despite their behavior), your Heavenly Father loves you with a depth of love you cannot fathom.

In Christ, you are a princess, a daughter of the Most High King. God has been using princess metaphors to teach me many things over the years. Here's another that speaks about honesty and identity.

In 1835, Hans Christian Andersen wrote a short fairy tale, *The Princess and the Pea.* In it, a bedraggled woman seeks shelter in a castle on a stormy night. We know little about her, except that despite her disheveled appearance, she declares she is a princess. You know the story. A tiny pea is put in her mattresses by a skeptical queen, the girl doesn't sleep well because of it, and in the morning, she honestly states that fact. Her honesty about her poor sleep reveals a deep sensitivity, thus confirming the girl's identity. This sensitive and honest young woman is a princess, just as she said.

The princess was honest about her misery in the night. Her honesty won her a prince. It's something to think about.

Set Out Toward Surrender

Read Hebrews 4:15-16. How does this give you confidence to be honest with God?

Reflect on your recent study and these verses. Write out what is stirring in your spirit as you bring the truth of God's Word into the landscape of your life.

Chapter Three Prayer and Promise

We have explored how Isaiah 30 reveals God's view of relationship with the people of Judah. He called them His children. If you have faith in Christ, you are also one of His children. There are differences between identities you may adopt and the identity you have as God's daughter. There can also be a disconnect between what you say and what you do.

We sometimes live out of things other than our true identities as beloved children of God. By comparing orphan thinking and beloved-daughter thinking, we can gain a window into our hearts. We must allow the Holy Spirit to guide us into truth and surrender.

There is more to learn about how we rest in intimate relationship with God. Our study of Isaiah 30 so far has revealed we need to:

- Recognize circumstances (Chapter One)
- Respond to invitation (Chapter Two)
- Recover your identity (Chapter Three)

These are foundations that enable us to rest in deeper relationship with God and experience the abundance He speaks of in Isaiah 30:15, John 10:10, and elsewhere in the Bible.

Children must grow into maturity within earthly families, and that is true of children in God's family as well. This is the process of sanctification. We are guided in sanctification by the Holy Spirit. He is faithful to help us see what is standing in the way of recognizing, responding, and receiving.

You can recover and walk in your identity as a beloved child of God.

Key Practice: Ask the Lord to help you identify where you may not be living fully in your identity as God's beloved daughter. Begin by listing any areas of orphan mindset you discovered through self-reflection in this chapter. Meditate on the Scriptures from Lessons Three and Four. Look for the truths of Scripture speaking to your specific places of need.

Key Promise: "And I am certain that God, who began the good work within you, will continue his work until it is finally finished on the day when Christ Jesus returns."

Philippians 1:6 (NLT)

Heavenly Father, I come to you grateful that in Christ I am your beloved child. Thank you for pursuing me even when I am living out of false identities or fear. Continue to reveal to me more of who I am in Christ and give me grace to embrace the truth of how You see me. Give me courage to be honest and trusting of Your heart toward me. Thank you, Jesus.

Notes

Notes

Chapter Four: Refine Your Sensitivity

Key Idea: You can refine sensitivity to God's voice to increase intimacy with Him.

Key Verse: "Your own ears will hear him. Right behind you a voice will say, 'This is the way you should go,' whether to the right or to the left." Isaiah 30:21 (NLT)

We have spent the first half of our study working through roughly the first half of Isaiah 30. In this chapter, our lessons turn toward the latter half of the book, specifically exploring verses 18-22 for the next two chapters.

Deepened intimacy with God comes as you attend to the things we have studied: recognizing your circumstances, responding to God's invitation, and recovering your identity as His beloved child. That foundation allows you to rest in Him. But we are on a journey toward more of Him. Cultivation of truly intimate relationship with God is possible through the Holy Spirit living within you. What are the qualities and characteristics of this intimate relationship? That is what we will explore in the remainder of our study.

Consider the princess from *The Princess and the Pea*. She was so sensitive she was able to detect a tiny pea in a giant stack of mattresses. When she was tested in this way, her identity was revealed and confirmed. Her sensitivity made all the difference.

Our intimacy with God increases when we have sensitivity in two different directions:
- to Him and His voice
- to the obstacles which rob us of rest in Him

This chapter focuses on the first facet of sensitivity: refining our sensitivity to God and His voice. As we continue studying Isaiah 30, we will encounter truths that enable us to increase our capacity for sensitivity to the Lord.

Lesson One: The Father Who Waits

O loving God, Jesus, Holy Spirit, come into my time of study today. Give me eyes to see and ears to hear what you desire to show me in your Word.

A Voice of Love

Whether you realize it or not, you probably read Scripture with a particular tone of voice in your mind. For years, when I read Old Testament prophecy, God had a harsh, judgmental tone of voice in my head. Thankfully, God has broadened my perspective over the years as I have come to know Him better.

Read Isaiah 30:1-5 and 12-17 aloud, if you can. Imagine God's words being spoken with the voice of a grief-filled parent longing for the best for His children. How does imagining this tone of voice affect how you hear these words?

How does that impact your perception of God?

Making a Turn Toward Intimacy

Isaiah 30:18 marks a notable shift. The verses you just read aloud are presented as a direct quotation in the first-person voice of God. At verse 18, there is a shift to the voice of Isaiah as narrator. For the rest of the chapter, Isaiah speaks of God in the third person. He declares things about God rather than presenting the specific words of God. But this is no less authoritative. Isaiah is, after all, God's anointed prophet (Isaiah 6). As such, Isaiah is, as one theologian describes: "God's Spirit-endowed [servant] and [spokesman]."[14]

There is another shift in verse 18. The tone of the text moves away from one of indictment to a message of hope and opportunity.

Read Isaiah 30:18. What words stand out to you as you read this verse?

---

[14] Clendenen, E. Ray. "Introduction to the Old Testament Prophets." *Everyday Study Bible*, Holman Bible Publishers, Brentwood, TN, 2018, pp. 846–849.

Translations vary, depending on whether it is a more word-for-word or thought-for-thought translation of the Hebrew. Since we will be looking at four specific words, we will use the more word-for-word New American Standard Bible for the activity below. Find that translation of Isaiah 30:18 (there are plenty online) and fill in the missing words:

"Therefore the LORD _____ to be _____ to you,

And therefore He _____ on high to have _____ on you.

For the LORD is a God of justice; How blessed are all those who long for Him."

What do you notice about the word *LORD* in the first line? Which Hebrew name of God is being used? (Look back at Chapter Two, Lesson Two if you can't remember.)

What verb goes in the first blank in line one?

What verb goes in the first blank in line two?

God Is Longing and Waiting

The first verb, *longs*, is a Hebrew word meaning "to wait for, or long for."[15] It also has the sense of abiding and persevering. God is longing and waiting patiently for us. The second verb, *waits,* has a variety of meanings in Hebrew, including "to rise, rise up, be high, be lofty, be exalted."[16] For this reason, the Hebrew word is expressed "waits on high" in the NASB translation.

Verse 18 says God longs for us and waits to engage with us. What is He waiting for? Look at the first word of the verse. *Therefore* is a word indicating a conclusion is being drawn. It calls attention to what has come before, specifically verses 15-17, which include the detail of Judah running away from God's invitation.

---

[15] "H2442 - Ḥāḵâ - Strong's Hebrew Lexicon (ESV)." *Blue Letter Bible*, www.blueletterbible.org/lexicon/h2442/esv/wlc/0-1/.

[16] Outline of Biblical Usage. "H7311 - Rûm - Strong's Hebrew Lexicon (ESV)." *Blue Letter Bible*, www.blueletterbible.org/lexicon/h7311/esv/wlc/0-1/.

While many translations don't explicitly express the connection to the previous verses, the New Living Translation of Isaiah 30:18 does: "So the Lord must wait *for you to come to him* so he can show you his love and compassion. For the Lord is a faithful God. Blessed are those who wait for his help." (Emphasis added.)

What is This Waiting God Like?

God is longing for and waiting for His children to return to Him. Why? Verse 18 supplies two reasons.

God is gracious and compassionate. Write out below your own definitions for these words, including as many synonyms as you can for each.

What is your definition of *gracious?*

How do you define *compassionate?*

How are these words similar?

How are they different from each other?

According to *Strong's Hebrew Lexicon*, the Hebrew word translated *gracious* in verse 18 includes the meaning "to bend or stoop in kindness to an inferior."[17] I love this picture of God bending in kindness to meet me where I am.

---

[17] "H2603 - Ḥānan - Strong's Hebrew Lexicon (ESV)." *Blue Letter Bible*, www.blueletterbible.org/lexicon/h2603/esv/wlc/0-1/.

The Hebrew word translated *compassion* is also a rich word with several ways to be translated, including: "to love, love deeply, have mercy, be compassionate, have tender affection, have compassion."[18]

Which meanings for either *gracious* or *compassion* most resonate with you?

Gracious and *compassionate* are used other places God describes Himself. The same Hebrew roots appear in the passage below, where God reveals more about His name to Moses. After securing Moses safely in the cleft of a rock (Exodus 33:18-23), God passes by and proclaims His identity to Moses:

> The LORD passed in front of him and proclaimed: "The LORD —the LORD is a compassionate and gracious God, slow to anger and abounding in faithful love and truth." (Exodus 34:6 CSB)

What are the five different words and phrases God uses to describe Himself?

Which of these descriptions appeals to you most? Why do you think that is?

Notice again the three uses of *LORD* in Exodus 34:6. These are more instances of *YHWH*. God connecting five different descriptions of Himself to the personal name *YHWH* adds to our understanding of His intimate nature.

This is the present, patient God who waits on us to return to Him, to stop running away and trying to do things in our own strength. He is faithfully waiting for us to accept His invitation to intimacy.

---

[18] "H7355 - Rāḥam - Strong's Hebrew Lexicon (ESV)." *Blue Letter Bible*, www.blueletterbible.org/lexicon/h7355/esv/wlc/0-1/.

Lesson Two: Blessed Are Those Who Wait

O loving God, Jesus, Holy Spirit, come into my time of study today. Give me eyes to see and ears to hear what you desire to show me in your Word.

Waiting on God

Isaiah 30:18 reveals God's faithfulness and great patience with His wayward children. He is longing to show mercy to those who will turn their faces toward Him. This verse also ends with the picture of a believer waiting for God.

Bible commentator David Guzik offers insight on this verse and on waiting: "We often wonder why the LORD waits to do things in our lives. Isaiah tells us plainly that it is so He may be gracious to you. Whenever the LORD waits or seems to delay, it always has a loving purpose behind it. We can trust that even when we don't understand it."[19]

It may have appeared to the ancient Judeans that God was never going to come through for them in the face of the Assyrian threat. Indeed, they had given up on Him, turning their trust and attention to the lesser god of Egypt. In our own lives, we may be tempted to "give up" on God, especially if we have been waiting many years to see Him act. Delay isn't always denial, however.

Read 2 Peter 3:8-9. What are your experiences with waiting on God?

How do Guzik's words and the verses in 2 Peter 3 impact your perspective on waiting?

Instant Everything

Isaiah 30:18 ends with this phrase: "Blessed are all those who wait for him" (ESV). Waiting is not our favorite thing. It is very counter-cultural. We live in an instant gratification world.

---

[19] Guzik, David. "Study Guide for Isaiah 30." *Blue Letter Bible*, www.blueletterbible.org/comm/guzik_david/study-guide/isaiah/isaiah-30.cfm?a=709018.

Read Matthew 4:1-4. What was the first temptation Jesus faced after 40 days of fasting in the wilderness?

What was His response?

The first thing the devil threw at Jesus was the temptation to instant gratification. Jesus was doubtless hungry; turning stones to bread might seem a reasonable thing. But Jesus wouldn't be snared by the tyranny of the urgent. He rejected that temptation with the Word of God. His perspective was oriented around God rather than His own fleshly need.

What are some ways you encounter the "tyranny of the urgent" in your own life?

How does your response to those temptations compare to Christ's?

What a challenge it is to learn to live on God's timetable in our "instant everything" world. This is why I need as much unity and intimacy with Him as I can get. As He sanctifies me, He slows me to live on His timetable instead of the one offered by the world, my own flesh, or the temptations of the enemy.

Blessed are Those Who Wait

Have you ever seen a toddler throw a temper tantrum in public because he or she was on a different timetable than a parent? It isn't a good look. Sometimes I am like that when faced with waiting or not getting my own way. As an adult, I have managed to keep from flinging myself on the floor and wailing in public, but inside can be a different, fuming story. If I am waiting, it often means I am not getting my own way exactly when I want to get it. That doesn't always feel like a blessing, but in Isaiah 30:18, God says it is.

Waiting involves humility. Whether you are waiting on the Lord or in a line at the DMV, waiting well requires putting aside your "self" and its desires. Humility is a crucial step in the surrender required for experiencing more of Him. It opens the door wider to the blessing of more of His sanctifying work.

Read Psalm 25:3. What is the blessing for those who wait?

Read Psalm 40:1-3. What blessings did David encounter by waiting on God?

Read Proverbs 20:22. What blessing for waiting is mentioned here?

Read Isaiah 40:31. What blessings are given to those who wait on God?

Read Lamentations 3:25-26. What is the blessing here?

No shame. Rescue and firm ground to stand on. Praises to sing. Deliverance. Renewed strength. Salvation. Yes, "blessed are all those who wait for him" (Isaiah 30:18 ESV).

All good relationships take time to cultivate and develop. As intimacy increases, patience and grace are always required on the part of both parties. God is waiting to be gracious to us. Will we wait on Him?

Lesson Three: God Guides

O loving God, Jesus, Holy Spirit, come into my time of study today. Give me eyes to see and ears to hear what you desire to show me in your Word.

Prophetic Shift

Recall the shift at Isaiah 30:18 from God speaking in the first person to Isaiah's narration about God? Another shift at that verse is to a more hopeful tone about the future. In the remainder of the chapter, Isaiah speaks about specific, restorative events in Jerusalem's near future. He also expresses everlasting characteristics of God, such as His presence, His victory over oppression, and His blessings. One way to reap benefit from prophetic writings is to see how their details are borne out by the rest of God's Word.

Read Isaiah 30:20-21. Outline below the key principles or promises you find.

There are three main principles:
- You will have hard things.
- You will have guidance.
- Your guide will be present with you.

We Will Have Hard Times

We examined hard circumstances in Chapter One, so we won't spend too long here now. It is, however, worth noting one commentator's insight on verse 20: "[God] intended the hardship [His children] were experiencing to turn them back to him!"[20] Indeed, God is always pointing us back to Himself, even if it requires allowing hard things into our lives.

Read John 16:33. What does Jesus say we will have?

---

[20] Beyer, Bryan E. *Encountering the Book of Isaiah*, Baker Academic, Grand Rapids, MI, 2007, pp. 127.

Why does He tell us to take heart or have courage?

Read Hebrews 12:3-11. Think of what you've studied about your identity as a child of God. What relationship is expressed in this passage between hardships, discipline, and identity?

What does verse 11 promise us is the fruit of training in our lives?

You Will Have Guidance

Read Isaiah 30:20-21. What two senses are mentioned here?

What will they detect?

We are told in these verses we will see and hear our teacher. What comes to mind when you think of "guidance from God?"

Read Psalm 25:4-5. What is David asking God to do for him?

Read Psalm 25:8-10. What is David's testimony concerning God's guidance?

Read John 16:13. What does Jesus promise about the Holy Spirit?

Read Colossians 1:9-10. What does the apostle Paul pray for on behalf of believers?

All these verses assume a significant fact: God is available and willing to offer guidance to His children. This confidence in God's guidance is spread across thousands of years of history. David lived more than a thousand years before Jesus and Paul. The witness of Christian history since Jesus' days attests to the continuing guidance of God. Why wouldn't we expect it from Him today? Below, compose your own prayer concerning guidance you would like to have from God.

A Word Behind You

Read Isaiah 30:21. Where is the voice or word located in relation to the hearer?

Preacher Charles Spurgeon described God's mercy and grace as calling out from behind those who have turned their backs to Him, as Isaiah 30:21 suggests. Spurgeon says:

> Yet the Lord follows him, and with a voice of touching love and tender compassion he calls to him. . . . Again and again the wise, earnest, personal voice assails his ear, as if love resolved that he should not perish if wooing could win him to life. The wanderer seeks not God, but his God seeks him. Man turns from the God of love, but the love of God turns not away from him.[21]

---

[21] Spurgeon, C. H. "The Voice Behind Thee." *Blue Letter Bible*, 18 Apr. 1970, www.blueletterbible.org/comm/spurgeon_charles/sermons/1672.cfm?a=709022.

This theme of pursuit is seen throughout Isaiah 30. Even as God is calling out warning and indictment against His children, He is pursuing them with invitations of love and assurances of guidance. He is wooing us too.

Your Guide Will Be with You

Isaiah 30:20-21 also can be taken as a pointing forward—not only to the earthly ministry of Christ, but to the ministry of His Spirit living in Christ's followers. Look again at these verses. When will one's ears hear God's voice?

Translations differ slightly, but this is clear: God's voice of guidance is present in our comings and goings, and it is near enough for us to hear. This is specific, turn-by-turn navigation from a presence right with you. That sounds a lot like the Holy Spirit living inside believers.

In Chapter Two, Lesson Four, we looked at passages in John 14 and John 16 about the mission and ministry of the Holy Spirit. You may want to review what you learned there. Other New Testament passages are filled with additional information about the Spirit's guidance. I suggest reading passages such as Romans 8:5-17 and 26-27 or 1 Corinthians 2:6-16 to learn more about the Holy Spirit and His guidance.

Trust He is at work as you seek more of Him.

Lesson Four: See and Hear

O loving God, Jesus, Holy Spirit, come into my time of study today. Give me eyes to see and ears to hear what you desire to show me in your Word.

This is the Way

I don't think I've ever met anyone who enjoys the sensation of feeling lost or unsure. Even free-spirited adventurers will eventually long for a little direction. As believers in Christ, we especially long for the guidance of God.

Within the Star Wars franchise is a series called *The Mandalorian*. A catchphrase from the show emerged: "This is the way." In that fictional universe, "this is the way" is an affirmation of the moral code and traditions of the warrior-like Mandalorian characters.

Of course, God got there way before Hollywood and Star Wars. In many translations, Isaiah 30:21 contains the exact phrase: "This is the way." The relationship described in the second half of Isaiah 30 is beautiful because it is personal, restful, and filled with protection. Yet so many things war against this intimacy. Sometimes we struggle to see and hear, to wait well, and to trust.

Seeing and Hearing

Ancient Judah also struggled mightily to wait upon and trust God. Their struggle had to do with what they could see and what they could hear, or, rather, what they were *willing* to see and hear.

Read Isaiah 30:9-11, printed below. Circle words you find related to the senses of seeing and hearing or to the phrase "the way."

> For they are a rebellious people, lying children, children unwilling to hear the instruction of the Lord; who say to the seers, 'Do not see,' and to the prophets, 'Do not prophesy to us what is right; speak to us smooth things, prophesy illusions, leave the way, turn aside from the path, let us hear no more about the Holy One of Israel' (ESV).

Compare Isaiah 30:9-11 to Isaiah 30:20-21. What contrasts do you observe?

In the first passage, God calls out Judah for a lack of seeing and hearing, for walking away from His paths. In the second, He promises He can be seen, can be heard, and He affirms the value of His ways. The theme of hearing and seeing runs throughout the Bible. Isaiah references it often, perhaps because of the specific message God gave him as a prophet.

Read Isaiah 6:9-10. What is God's specific message to Judah through Isaiah?

By the time God anointed Isaiah, His people had long struggled to be faithful to Him. For centuries they had run away from Him toward lesser gods. God's message through Isaiah is what we might call "giving Judah a taste of their own medicine."

Isaiah 6:9-10 contains a paradox. God commands His people to see and hear but tells them they won't be able to. Why? Commentator Bryan Beyer notes: "The Lord's instruction contained within it the idea that the people of Judah were not yet ready to respond fully to God's message. . . . They had deep spiritual lessons to learn. Once they learned these lessons, they would find his arms open to them."[22]

Absurdity and Blind Guides

Read Psalm 135:15-18. What do you learn here about seeing and hearing? What do you learn about people who make and trust in idols?

Psalm 135:18 says those who trust in idols become deaf, mute, and dead, just as idols are. This is part of what Beyer calls "deep spiritual lessons" Judah had to learn. They pursued deadness, while God offered life through relationship. How heartrending for Him to watch His beloved children run after things He knows cannot satisfy them.

---

[22] Beyer, Bryan E. "Oracles of Woe." *Encountering the Book of Isaiah*, Baker Academic, Grand Rapids, MI, 2007, p. 66.

The Call Continues

Jesus quoted Isaiah 6:9-10. It is recorded in all four gospels (Matthew 13:13-15, Mark 4:12, Luke 8:10, John 12:39-40). When Jesus references Isaiah 6, He draws a contrast between those who have engaged in relationship with Him and those who haven't.

Read Matthew 13:10-16. What do the disciples ask Jesus about?

What does He say about the difference between those who understand parables and those not understanding them?

What is the role of intimacy with Jesus in that difference?

Inside the Kingdom of God, for those in relationship with Jesus, the gift of seeing, hearing, and understanding are present. Outside relationship with Him there is confusion, spiritual blindness, and deafness.

The apostle Paul also quotes the Isaiah 6 prophecy (Acts 28:25-27). Arriving in Rome, Paul shares the gospel with Jewish leaders. Some believed, others did not (Acts 28:17-28). Beyer concludes: "In each generation down through the centuries, people exist who hear God's truth and reject it. When they do, they fulfill Isaiah's words again. But others hear it, accept it, and thus receive more."[23]

Matthew 13:12 records Jesus assuring this principle: "For to the one who has, more will be given, and he will have an abundance, but from the one who has not, even what he has will be taken away" (ESV).

The Message renders the same passage: "Whenever someone has a ready heart for this, the insights and understandings flow freely. But if there is no readiness, any trace of receptivity soon disappears" (MSG). May we have eyes to see and ears to hear.

---

[23] Beyer, Bryan E. "Oracles of Woe." *Encountering the Book of Isaiah*, Baker Academic, Grand Rapids, MI, 2007, p. 68.

Lesson Five: Sensitivity Training: Loud Voices, Lenses, Lies

O loving God, Jesus, Holy Spirit, come into my time of study today. Give me eyes to see and ears to hear what you desire to show me in your Word.

I Didn't Get Much Rest

Several years ago, my son's friend spent the night with us. When asked how he slept, he reported he had struggled. Apparently, the train had kept him up. Across a pasture behind our house are train tracks crossing three roads within a tenth of a mile. When a train comes through, its horn blasts repeatedly for nearly 45 seconds. Our guest's sleep was disrupted several times by it.

We've lived in this house for more than two decades. I have become so used to the nightly cacophony, I don't even notice it. My son's friend had a sensitivity I didn't. He hadn't been worn down by years of acclimation.

Remember *The Princess and the Pea*? She couldn't sleep either. Like our guest, she was sensitive to something that robbed her of rest. We can learn from these examples.

In Isaiah 30:20-21, God says we will see Him and hear His voice. So why do we sometimes struggle with this?

Perhaps we have lost sensitivity, like me with the train. Maybe we have become so accustomed to certain things that we have lost some capacity for hearing or seeing. Obstacles stand in the way of our sensitivity to the voice of the Spirit and His guidance.

An old saying names enemies of intimacy with God as "the world, the flesh, and the devil." Another way to describe these enemies is loud voices, lenses, and lies. The world is filled with loud voices, our flesh adopts its own skewed lenses or perspectives, and the enemy lies, like He always has. Jesus alluded to these obstacles in the parable of the sower in Matthew 13.

Loud Voices of the World

Read Matthew 13:7 and 13:22. Where did this seed fall according to verse 7?

What does Jesus reveal about the thorns choking the seed in verse 22?

Vast amounts of information compete for our attention from the moment we wake up each day. The world reverberates with shouting, both literally and figuratively. Loud voices wrench our attention away from God as we try to sort out all the noise.

What types of voices draw your attention? Consider these questions as a start:
- What types of social media posts catch your attention?

- What sections of a news feed do you slow down to read?

- What sort of advertising impacts you most?

- What influenced you to make your last major purchase?

- What do you daydream about?

- What do you worry about?

Lenses of the Flesh

Read Matthew 13:5-6 and 13:20-21. Where did this seed fall according to verse 5?

How did Jesus describe a person who is like the rocky soil in verses 20-21?

Understanding the lenses through which you view the world is critical. Getting our words and our hearts in alignment with His is a key to intimacy with God. This takes time and attention. It involves persistence that not everyone desires to pursue. Recall Judah's desire for easy, pleasant, smooth things instead of what was right (Isaiah 30:10). This is the human condition.

We are all born with what the Bible sometimes calls "the flesh." This is our nature, marred by sin, which is oriented to see everything through the lens of our personal desires. This sin nature makes us all want to choose self over Savior. Most of us desire easy, comfortable things.

When we are redeemed by Christ, we have victory over that flesh. We can see through the lens of God rather than the lens of our flesh. But we can still wrestle with the old nature. Even the apostle Paul struggled with this (Romans 7:15-25). One pastor I know calls it getting stuck in "stinking thinking."

When God asked me to break up with Wonder Woman, He showed me I often had the wrong person on the throne of my heart; I wasn't rooted in Him. My path to healing started with seeing the faulty lens I was looking through and living from.

Read Romans 8:5-6. What does the lens of the flesh pursue?

What about the lens of the Spirit?

Consider whether a lens of the flesh or of the Spirit has more of your attention. Here are some questions to help:

- Are you more focused on problem solving or striving than waiting on God?

- Are you more focused on what you lack than in confidence in God's abundance?

- Are you more focused on blame of self or others than worship of Jesus?

- Are you more focused on complaint or praise?

- Do you have trouble asking for or accepting help?

- Are you more independent or dependent?

- Are your eyes more on your circumstances than they are on your Savior?

Lies of the Enemy

Read Matthew 13:3-4 and 13:19. What happened to these seeds according to verse 4? How does Jesus explain this in verse 19?

From the opening of Genesis, the Bible makes clear we have an enemy. The Bible is also very clear about his nature.

Read John 8:44. How does Jesus describe the devil?

The father of lies assails us with half-truths and lies, usually disguised as things that sound pretty good. "If you dream it, you can do it" or "You've got this!" or "Live your truth," to name just a few. Those lies all lead to the dead end of independence from God. We would do well to consider the reality and impact of the father of lies, just as Jesus did. The next chapter will help equip you for that.

The Fourth Seed

Jesus mentions a fourth seed in the parable of the sower: "As for what was sown on good soil, this is the one who hears the word and understands it. He indeed bears fruit . . ." (Matthew 13:23a ESV).

After a lesson on all these obstacles, you might be tempted to discouragement, thinking you will never be that fourth type of seed. We close, then, with a word of encouragement from the last prayer Jesus prayed before going to the cross for you.

Read John 17:14-20. Take special note of verse 20, just in case you are tempted to think this prayer isn't specifically for you.

Chapter Four Prayer and Promise

In this chapter we've seen the promise of guidance and intimacy with God as we walk along the paths of life. Within this intimate relationship, we should expect to see and hear Him through the guidance of His Spirit and His Word.

We will face obstacles to intimacy with Christ, and they generally come in three realms: the world's loud voices, our own lenses, and the enemy's lies. There isn't a clear line between where one of these obstacles ends and another begins. Loud voices are often filled with lies, our perspectives can be influenced by the loud voices of others or by the lies of the enemy. We must recognize this trio of influences warring against sensitivity to God.

In the next chapter, we will move into some strategies to combat these desensitizing influences. To prepare, I encourage you to engage in the Key Practice below: asking God questions and listening for His answer. Isaiah 30:20-21 promises we can see and hear Him. Take some time to press deeper into that. Start small if this is new for you. Choose one of the questions below. Ask it. Then listen for an answer. It really is that simple. Sometimes an answer comes in an immediate impression; it might come through His Word or through something another person says. Don't be discouraged if you struggle with this. Like any new skill, it will take practice. The thing is to step out in faith.

You can refine sensitivity to God's voice to increase intimacy with Him.

Key Practice: Ask God a question or two and listen for His answer. Here are some ideas to start with as you practice listening to His voice:

- God, what is something about You I am desensitized to?
- God, what is something robbing me of resting in You?
- God, what is something that has stolen my identity as your beloved daughter?
- God, what is one thing robbing me of intimacy with You?

Key Promise: "I will instruct you and teach you in the way you should go; I will counsel you with my loving eye on you."

Psalm 32:8 (NIV)

Father, thank you that you don't hide yourself from me. I am grateful your Word teaches me I can trust your Spirit is at work. Thank you that I don't have to fix myself. Give me grace to be as willing to wait for you as you are willing to wait for me. Help me to hear you more clearly. Thank you for the hope that is in me through Jesus Christ.

Notes

Notes

Chapter Five: Reject Idols and Obstacles

Key Idea: You can reject obstacles to intimacy with God.

Key Verse: "Then you will defile your carved idols overlaid with silver and your gold-plated metal images. You will scatter them as unclean things. You will say to them, 'Be gone!'"

Isaiah 30:22 (ESV)

These next lessons center around this chapter's Key Verse. Christians today don't talk a lot about idolatry, but understanding it is a critical component to finding rest and deepening intimacy with God.

Another focus in this chapter is on practices to help you identify and reject the obstacles warring against your intimacy with God. At the end of each lesson, you'll see a section titled **Trust the Process**, followed by a specific practice to try.

"Trust the Process" is a slogan I first encountered as a kid. The phrase stuck in my head. Trusting God's processes, I've found, is a hallmark of finding His peace within the chaos of this world. I would call "the process" a part of sanctification.

Sanctification, or being transformed by God, is relational and there are rhythms to it. As you study these next five lessons, you'll encounter five practices. These practices can open you to the work of the Spirit, but they are by no means the only practices God uses to sanctify us. These steps can be significant, however, in increasing your sensitivity to what stands in the way of more intimacy with God.

Don't get tricked into relying on your own efforts. The gospel is based on the truth we can never be "good enough" or ever "get our act together" enough. Our self-created "righteousness" is like filthy rags to God (Isaiah 64:6).

Tension exists here. We have things to do. We cooperate with the Holy Spirit and place ourselves before God. We invite Him in. We let Him lead. Yet He is also inviting us. He initiates, empowers, and imparts all that bears fruit in us. We know God has a process and that it is good. But we don't control it. We must trust Him. All healthy, intimate relationships require trust. It is no different with the Lord.

Lesson One: Pray for Sensitivity

O loving God, Jesus, Holy Spirit, come into my time of study today. Give me eyes to see and ears to hear what you desire to show me in your Word.

Idols and Relationships

Read Isaiah 30:22. What is the first word of the verse?

What does this word signal about the relationship of this verse to the verses preceding it?

In most translations the first word of verse 22 is either *then* or *and*. Either conjunction expresses a relationship between this verse and what came before. Look back at verses 20-21. What do these verses concern?

Defiling and scattering idols comes *after* the hearing and seeing. We are not instructed to get rid of idols first so then we will be able to hear and see God. The sense in this passage is more that when we begin hearing and seeing God, we will want to get rid of anything false that stands between us.

Think about that. We so often believe we must get our act together and tidy up before coming to God or before we can expect anything from Him. We can get trapped in guilt which shames us into believing He doesn't want anything to do with us.

This is not the order of things here. Just as we have seen before in our study, God pursues His wayward children, even when they are worshiping idols.

What is an Idol?

If we hear anything about idols today, it is in the context of something like the singing show *American Idol* or in reference to a sports hero. According to *Merriam Webster*, an idol is "an object of extreme devotion."[24] True enough.

But how is *idol* defined biblically? According to *Smith's Bible Dictionary*, there are 21 different Hebrew words for idols or images for worship. "All of these terms expressed

---

[24] "Idol Definition & Meaning." *Merriam-Webster*, www.merriam-webster.com/dictionary/idol.

worthlessness and vanity, contempt and abhorrence."[25] That is a very different definition than what popular culture might say. We can try to remake the word *idol* with less harsh definitions, but that doesn't change God's view of idolatry.

Read each of the passages below. Notice especially how idolatry is compared with other things and the contexts in which idolatry is mentioned. What do you learn?

Exodus 20:3-6

1 Corinthians 5:9-11

Ephesians 5:5-6

Colossians 3:5

1 Peter 4:3-5

1 John 5:20-21

"The Bible understands that idolatry extends beyond the worship of images and false gods. It is a matter of the heart, associated with pride, self-centeredness, greed, gluttony, and a love for possessions,"[26] notes *Baker's Evangelical Dictionary of Biblical Theology*.

If it is true that God never changes (Hebrews 13:8) and that He condemns idolatry, then we can assume idolatry is still a serious matter to Him today. It might be tempting to believe we are free from idolatry because we don't bow down to carved images or statues. But are we? Consider again the words of Exodus 20:3. Wouldn't it be fair to think of an idol as anything allowed to take the place of God as king of your heart or take His place as the object of your worship?

---

[25] Smith, W. *Smith's Bible Dictionary*. Holman Bible Publishers, 1990.
[26] Elwell, Walter. "Idol, Idolatry - Baker's Evangelical Dictionary of Biblical Theology." *StudyLight.org*, www.studylight.org/dictionaries/eng/bed/i/idol-idolatry.html. 1996.

Closer to Home

We would do well to consider the issue of idolatry in our lives. We might have more in common with God's rebellious children in Isaiah 30 than we think. God has been guiding me to identify and reject idols in recent years. While it is a humbling experience, He is always very gentle in the way He leads me to see truth, reject lies, and embrace Him more. There is great freedom down this path.

He loves you so much! He wants you to be as sensitive as the princess with her pea, detecting and rejecting anything that has slipped into your life that would rob you of resting in Him. Here are some questions for your consideration.

How would you define an idol?

What is the relationship between idols, rest, and intimacy with God?

What in your life might stand in the way of deeper, more intimate relationship with God?

In what ways does the world around you, your flesh, or the enemy contribute to the temptation to idolatry? (Think back to the last lesson on the obstacles of loud voices, lenses, and lies.)

Trust the Process: Pray for Sensitivity

Throughout this chapter, we will end each lesson with a specific practice which can help us grow in sensitivity to God and in intimacy with Him. Each lesson will add a new step to this rhythm of relational intimacy.

You may not have specific insight into things that tempt you to rest in a lesser god than your Heavenly Father, but most of us have a general idea of where our temptations and struggles are. As Isaiah 30:20-21 teaches, God will give you guidance, even when you are in places of adversity and affliction. He will not leave you on your own.

The first step: Pray. Ask God to give you sensitivity to His voice and His Spirit. You have already started this if you worked through the Key Practice at the end of Chapter Four. (If not, peek back there and look.) Write out your prayer below.

Lesson Two: The Art of Paying Attention

O loving God, Jesus, Holy Spirit, come into my time of study today. Give me eyes to see and ears to hear what you desire to show me in your Word.

There are *P's* in My Mattress

After I broke up with Wonder Woman (Chapter Three, Lesson Five), I started praying Romans 12:2 regularly, asking God to transform and renew my mind. Shortly afterward, He led me to *The Princess and the Pea* fairy tale as a spiritual analogy. I began to discover "peas" in my own life—things that robbed me of resting in God and of freedom to walk in my identity as His beloved daughter.

Almost all these freedom and rest robbers are heart issues which are rightly called idols. In my case, nearly all of them start with the letter *P*. Performing, pride, people pleasing, and protecting myself are some of my most pronounced temptations. I'm a princess with a mattress full of *P's*.

You could call my *P's* by any number of names—sins, strongholds, obstacles, or idols. They are all fed by things we studied in the last chapter: the loud voices of the world, the lenses my flesh wants to look through, and the lies of the enemy. These three instigators work together to push me in directions other than to the Lord. I can relate to the people we've studied in Isaiah 30.

Defiling Images or Alliances?

Two nouns in the original language of the first sentence of Isaiah 30:22 are most often translated as *idols* and *images*. The ESV reads, ". . . your carved idols overlaid with silver and gold-plated metal images." The words *idols* and *images* sound like synonyms in English.

However, the words *metal images* and *alliance* probably don't sound like synonyms to you. Yet those words share the same Hebrew word, *masseka*. In Isaiah 30:22, *masseka* is translated "metal images," and it is translated "alliance" in Isaiah 30:1 in the ESV.[27] There is a root-word relationship between metal images and alliances.

Read Isaiah 30:1-2. What are God's complaints about Judah?

---

[27] "H4541 - Massēḵâ - Strong's Hebrew Lexicon (ESV)." *Blue Letter Bible*, www.blueletterbible.org/lexicon/h4541/esv/wlc/0-1/.

Read Isaiah 30:3-5, 7. What kind of help is this alliance going to be?

Idolatry in the Bible goes far beyond gold and silver statues; it is based on the alliances we make. Idolatry is always an issue of the heart. When your heart makes an alliance with something not of God's Spirit, you are engaging in the same thing He warned His children about in Isaiah 30. Idolatry is always an empty and worthless dead end, even if the thing we idolize seems good or "no big deal."

We are pretty good at spotting the "big no-no's" that drag us away from God. What we need more of is sensitivity to the subtle idolatry that entangles and enslaves. God started showing me where I was making agreements and alliances with empty things that could not profit me. I've got a whole list of *P's* to be on the lookout for, and I would not have seen them without God's leading. It is hard to defile the idols you don't know you have. The enemy would surely like you to stay right in that blind spot.

Trust the Process: Pay Attention to Pain Points

Today you'll add a second practice: paying attention to your pain points. The practice of paying attention has been woven throughout this study, so you've been practicing this skill already. By taking a deep dive into one chapter of Scripture, you've paid attention to definitions, context, and relationships between ideas. You've started attending to yourself by assessing your circumstances (Chapter One) and paying attention to your response to an invitation and identity from God (Chapters Two and Three).

It's time to take the next step: paying attention to your pain. Lies are at the root of most of our pain. Just like the queen in *The Princess and the Pea* assumed the pea in the mattresses would go undetected, our enemy wants to keep his lies shielded from our sight. But you don't have to settle for that. We can discover the subtle ways our hearts want to drift away from God. It starts with simply paying attention. This is a holy endeavor. French philosopher and Christian mystic Simone Weil observed, "Attention, taken to its highest degree, is the same thing as prayer. It presupposes faith and love."[28]

When God started helping me unpack the mess of my *P's*, He led me to pay more attention to my pain points, specifically. I began to attend to things triggering negative behaviors and emotions in me. For example, when I find myself angry or frustrated, it is an

---

[28] Weil, Simone. "Attention and Will." Rohan Drape, rohandrape.net/ut/rttcc-text/Weil1952d.pdf.

opportunity for me to pay attention and start noticing that I am hurting. When I pay attention, I am laying groundwork to find out more. We will talk about that next lesson.

Today, practice simply paying attention. Start noticing things that impact you or that capture your attention or your emotions. You might see patterns or habits you hadn't realized. Below are some questions to give you a start. Write out whatever comes to mind. You don't have to answer all of them. You may discover a different question that is more related to you and your needs. The Holy Spirit will guide you.

What makes you angry?

What makes you sad?

What causes you anxiety?

What makes you fearful?

What causes you to feel shame or self-condemnation?

What causes you to feel stuck?

What causes you to feel hopeless?

Lesson Three: Spirit, Help Me Name the Lies

O loving God, Jesus, Holy Spirit, come into my time of study today. Give me eyes to see and ears to hear what you desire to show me in your Word.

False Fronts

A couple of interesting words in Isaiah 30:22 hold valuable insight for us.
Read Isaiah 30:22. How are idols and images described in the first sentence?

The gold and silver mentioned in this verse are described in most translations as an overlay, a plating, or a covering. Idols have a false front. Appearing rich and valuable on the outside, they were generally wood or stone on the inside. A beautiful covering obscured their true nature.
Read Habakkuk 2:18-19. How are idols described in this verse?

Where do idols come from according to this verse?

What is the author's point about this?

Old Testament idols are not the only things covered with a false front. In many circumstances, there is more (or less) than meets the eye. As you read the passages in the chart below, fill in what you find related to the concept of a false front and anything you learn about how to recognize truth.

	What is the false front?	**How can I recognize truth?**
Matthew 7:15-20		
2 Corinthians 11:13-15		

Idols can take different forms—a gold plated-wooden statue, a false teacher, or the idea that money or fame will bring you happiness. Whatever its form, idolatry always includes some twisted version of the truth.

Read 2 Corinthians 11:3. What is Paul's concern?

Where does deception take place according to this verse?

Uncovering falsehoods influencing our thoughts is just as important today as it was in Paul's day. All that glitters is not gold. How do we discern what is a veneer and what is truth? Read the verses below. Write out what each teaches about finding truth.

1 Corinthians 2:12, 14

Ephesians 1:17-19

Hebrews 5:14

As a child of the King, you have access to His unlimited resources for discernment, direction, and the strength to walk in truth.

Finding the Roots of the *P's*

The enemy, speaking his native language, loves to plant seeds of lies and half-truths in our minds (John 8:44). He hopes these lies will grow into full-blown enslavement, as they did in the garden of Eden (Genesis 3:1-7). Like the shiny, gold-plated idols we've studied, the rotten core of his lies eventually wreak havoc and disrupt intimacy with our Father.

In Lesson Two, you began paying attention to your pain points. Once I started that practice, I saw patterns. I asked the Holy Spirit to give me insight into what was behind repeated behaviors or habits. Over time and through prayer, I began to see truth. For each *P* in my life (like pride, performing, or people pleasing), I discovered lies that had taken root, orienting my thinking away from God.

This discovery process is "reverse engineering." You start at the pain point and work backwards through habits and behaviors to get to the lies and the wounds behind them.

Discovering root lies is a Holy Spirit-led work. You have begun this process, as you are praying for increased sensitivity and paying attention. The next practice is to present your discoveries to God for insight. Ask Him to expose lies and let Him lead you to unmask roots that drive dysfunction.

My Performing *P*

As I began paying attention, I started noticing my anger. It would boil up and explode, seemingly out of nowhere and usually all over people I love deeply. Asking God for insight, I discovered the anger was a result of frustration and helplessness I felt every time I failed to live up to my own expectations. If I appeared less competent, less thoughtful, or less "good" than I wanted to be, I would get very angry. I presented this to the Lord, asking Him to help me identify the lies that fed the anger.

He showed me my performing *P* is rooted in two lies. The first lie is, "You are required to be a responsible, reliable person." The second lie is, "There's no help coming; you are on your own."

These lies formed a lens through which I viewed the world. It went something like this: "I have to perform well to be loved by God and others, and I have to figure out how to do that on my own because no one will help me." Together, the lies and the perspective or lens created by them led me to an idol of performing as a way of self-protection.

An event in early 1977 cemented the broken view I had of myself and of God. My family had moved to Washington, DC, from the Deep South in 1975. I was bullied by classmates for much of the two years we lived there. The bullying culminated with a group of girls grabbing me during recess. They tied me up to a soccer goalpost with bandannas and left me there while the rest of the class continued to play soccer around me. I felt helpless and alone. I made my first alliance with Wonder Woman on that playground.

While I was tied to that goalpost, I made a vow I would never let anyone treat me like that again. I swore I would never again let myself be that vulnerable. I was sure I had done something to cause the continual mistreatment by classmates who I thought were my friends. Deep, wounding messages lodged in my little-girl heart. I had given that heart to Jesus the year before, but I was a baby Christian. Even though He eventually sent a single, brave classmate to show compassion and untie me, damage was done. My elementary school heart wasn't sure I could trust Him fully. It definitely felt it could not trust people who pretended to be my friends.

It was years before I understood the truth: I am not on my own; I don't have to perform or to be responsible for everything; and my actions were not responsible for the hurtful choices my classmates made. Over time, I had to let God restore me to truth: Not every offer of relationship is from someone who tricks you into trust, then hurts your heart. He doesn't treat me that way. I am invited to His side, I am His beloved daughter, and He takes good care of me. The lies of the enemy had stolen those truths from me. But only for a time.

Trust the Process: Present Findings for Insight

As you might imagine from the story above, there are layers to finding deeper freedoms and intimacy in Christ. You cannot tackle everything at once. The next practice is to present to God what you are noticing through the first two steps of prayer and paying attention. *Presenting* is just bringing what you've noticed to Him and asking Him to reveal what He wants to show you. You may already have something to present to the Lord for insight. This is the beginning of the "reverse engineering." God will help you see and name the lies and their roots. You can ask Him to give you specific words to express what they are. He will do it in His time.

A good summary for this practice is "bring it to the light, so it can take flight." The enemy of your soul will try to convince you it is fruitless or too painful to ask the Lord to reveal truth. The enemy works in the shadows and likes things to stay hidden.

Read Ephesians 5:8-11. What does verse 11 say to do to unfruitfulness and darkness?

Try to take one of the things you discovered in your answers to the questions at the end of the last lesson. Present it to the Lord today and ask for His insights. Record what He shows you.

Lesson Four: Put Off and Reject Lies

O loving God, Jesus, Holy Spirit, come into my time of study today. Give me eyes to see and ears to hear what you desire to show me in your Word.

Unholy Alliance

In the last lesson, I shared a story about making a vow when I was tied to a soccer goalpost in 1977. That was the first time I made an alliance with Wonder Woman. I shared in Chapter Three my surrendering that idol to God on a ladies' retreat many years later.

Read Isaiah 30:1. According to the last phrase of this verse, what is the result of Judah's choices?

Adding sin to sin is not something I am interested in. But that is what happens when I align myself with powers and plans that aren't of God. The Holy Spirit traced my performance *P* back to lies cemented that day on the playground. I realized how destructive alliances like that can be. Admiring a fictional character isn't a problem for most people, but for me it was a slow-working poison. I didn't stop at admiring Wonder Woman. I made a vow to be strong "like her" so that no one could hurt me like that again.

In my pain, I aligned myself with the lie that God had abandoned me as well as the lie that I could not trust Him. In my childhood hurt, I grabbed on to a popular TV character who seemed to be able to handle all her own problems. I traded my true identity as God's beloved child for a false identity based on lies. It shaped the lens I viewed my life through, and it was reinforced through the loud voices of the world. It was a bad trade. This lesson and the next one will explore trading lies for truth.

Breaking Agreements

Read Isaiah 30:22. What are the three verbs or actions listed? (In most translations the words *you will* precede these verbs.)

Translations vary, but all contain the ideas of a choice to defile, destroy, ruin, throw away, or scatter idols. Notice the last verb in the last sentence. It mentions a specific action: speaking.

We are told to say to our idols, "Be gone." Whenever God reveals an area of sin or idolatry in my life, He reminds me of the power of renouncing unholy alliances and agreements. Isaiah 30:22 paints a picture of literally speaking aloud, "Be gone," to lesser gods we've allied ourselves with. Verbally confessing sin out loud and renouncing unholy agreements is powerful.

Read Psalm 118:8-13. What places of refuge are compared in verses 8 and 9?

Which place of refuge is best?

What phrase is repeated in verses 10-12?

What power can "cut off" threats?

What are some things you feel surrounded, hounded, or threatened by?

When we studied identity in Chapter Three, we noted the supernatural battle going on in our broken world. There is a battle for your confidence in your identity, and there is a battle being waged for the allegiance of your heart. But there is great power "in the name of the LORD," according to Scripture.

Read 2 Corinthians 10:3-5. What does it describe?

What does verse 5 say you can destroy?

There is a connection here between destroying strongholds, arguments, and opinions raised against God and taking our thoughts captive to Christ. The battlefield is related to our thoughts. The war is for our minds and the things we believe. Bringing our thoughts to Jesus and letting Him capture us with His truth and draw us into obedience to Him is a critical part of resting in God.

Put Off Lies

Another way the Bible talks about this battle with arguments against God is in the language of "putting off."

Read Ephesians 4:17-24. What are some negative traits described in verses 17-19?

What are you told to put off in verse 22?

What are you told to put on in verse 24?

Read Hebrews 12:1. What are you to put aside, put off, or lay aside?

Read James 1:21. What is to be put away?

These are general categories of things to which we should say, "Be gone." The Bible contains several lists of specific areas to put off. (See Galatians 5:19-21, Ephesians 4:17-32, Colossians 3:8-9, among others.) If you have been working through the practices described at the end of each lesson in this chapter, you probably already have some ideas about what the Holy Spirit might be leading you to "put off." If not, keep talking with God about it.

Confidence and Power

God pursues us even when we are allied elsewhere. We have seen His compassion, mercy, and grace all through this study. Even so, when we confront stubborn habits or repeated sin in our lives, we can be tempted to discouragement. If you were indeed on your own, you would have cause for discouragement. In Christ, however, you have the power to find forgiveness, and to find victory over sin and all the powers seeking to keep you enslaved in it.

Read 1 John 4:4. What does this say about who is in you?

Read 1 John 1:9. What do you have when you confess your sins?

Trust the Process: Put Off and Reject Lies

God may already be drawing you to specific lies you need to reject. If that is the case, the next practice is to say to them, "Be gone." If you know a specific area or lie needing addressing, move forward into rejecting these things. Borrow language from Psalm 118 and speak aloud a "cutting off in the name of Jesus" to any lies you are believing. Or break alliances in a prayer of confession to God, confident He is willing and able to give you freedom and forgiveness.

Here is a simple prayer I've used: *Lord, I am so thankful for your love for me. I confess I have believed the lie that (fill in with your specifics). I reject that lie in the name of Jesus, and I renounce any agreements I have made with (specific lie). I break agreements I have made with anything that is not your truth. Forgive me for this (name any specifics of the sin or the agreements). I receive your forgiveness and mercy in the name of Jesus.*

If you are breaking agreements with things that have played a significant, controlling role in your life, I encourage you to share this work with a Christian friend or your faith community. You'll recall when I broke up with Wonder Woman at the ladies' retreat, I shared it with friends for accountability and support.

Finally, stay focused on the fact that these are areas in which you are being invited to freedom. They are not areas for self-condemnation or shame.

Read Romans 8:1. Speak it aloud. Declare it as truth over yourself.

Lesson Five: Put on Truth and Embrace Grace

O loving God, Jesus, Holy Spirit, come into my time of study today. Give me eyes to see and ears to hear what you desire to show me in your Word.

Restoration and Renewal

I have returned twice as an adult to the playground where I was tied to the soccer goalpost. The first time, in 2011, I was stunned to discover that after more than three decades, the soccer goal was still standing. I wept as I stood in that spot declaring forgiveness to kids who had bullied me years before. I was on holy ground both physically and in the healing God was beginning in my heart.

In 2018, I had the opportunity to go back. I was stunned once again. The entire playground had been transformed and re-landscaped. The place the goalposts once stood was now a garden, complete with a large, metal wind spinner, and planted with bushes that had attracted butterflies. Not a trace of the old soccer goals remained. The new life analogy was not lost on me. Tears again, but this time tears of pure joy at the creative and loving heart of God. He cemented something different more deeply in my heart that day: in the end He makes beauty even from places of ruin.

God is all about transformation and redemption, even in the landscapes (literal and metaphorical) that have contained great pain.

New Life in Truth

Read Isaiah 30:23-26. What sorts of things are depicted here?

How would you describe this imagery?

Once the idols are scattered, life and abundance can flow. These verses picture fruitfulness and health, abundance, and great light. These are pictures of redemption and restoration, which are themes throughout all of Scripture. God is on mission to make all things new (Revelation 21:5). This includes you!

According to 2 Corinthians 5:17: "Therefore, if anyone is in Christ, he is a new creation; the old has passed away, and see, the new has come!" (CSB).

In Christ, old things are dead, new life has arrived. John 10:10 also reveals Jesus reminding us of another contrast involving abundance. Write out the verse below.

"Put on" in the Power of the Holy Spirit

In the last lesson we looked briefly at 2 Corinthians 10:3-5 and supernatural weapons of warfare. Now let's add to that. Jesus purchased full life for you on the cross. You are not on your own to seek victory over the loud voices, lenses, and lies that want to keep you ensnared in half-truths and sin. In Christ you have powerful resources for putting on truth and walking in it.

Read Romans 13:11-14. What are you to put aside according to verse 12?

What are you to put on according to verse 12?

What does verse 14 tell you to put on?

Think about what you know from the Bible about light and about Jesus. What are some ways light and Jesus are connected?

Read John 8:12. What does Jesus say of Himself?

What is His promise to those who follow Him?

We studied the power of living "in Christ" in Chapter Three. We also talked about "wearing Christ," but it bears repeating: "Jesus Christ is the best clothing for Christians to adorn themselves with, [and] to arm themselves with," says commentator Matthew Henry.[29]

Armor Up

Several places in the New Testament give a deeper picture of the armor of God. These add additional context for what it looks like to walk "adorned and armed" in Christ.

Read 1 Thessalonians 5:8 and Ephesians 6:13-17. Use these verses to fill out the chart below, noting what spiritual weapon is represented by each piece of armor. (Note: some pieces represent more than one thing.)

Piece of Armor	Spiritual Weapon
Breastplate	
Helmet	
Something for the waist or a belt	
Something for the feet or shoes	
Shield	
Sword	

---

[29] Henry, Matthew. "Romans 13:12 - Verse-by-Verse Bible Commentary." *StudyLight.org*, www.studylight.org/commentary/romans/13-12.html.

Now Read Isaiah 59:17, which describes armor God wears. Add its pieces to the chart, using the two blank lines on the left to add two new items. Your filled-out chart reveals a comprehensive picture. When we are surrendered to and aligned with God, we have access to this tremendous arsenal of power and protection.

It would be quite tempting to look at the lists and the processes we've been talking about in these lessons and start feeling a lot of pressure to perform, to get things "right." Let's review some truth.

Read Isaiah 30:15. Where is your strength?

Write out a reminder to yourself of what God is inviting you to.

Trust the Process: Put on Truth and Embrace Grace

The final practice for this chapter on exposing and rejecting idols and obstacles is to "put on" truth. This practice positions you to receive His grace and to strengthen yourself in His truth. It is part of inviting His healing into places where you have discovered a "pea" in your mattress. For my *P* of performing, I have a couple of verses about God's grace I lean into for clarity. One of them is Isaiah 30:15.

There are numerous resources for finding scriptural truth to "put on." One simple method is to take the specific sin, lie, or agreement God has revealed to you and use an online search engine to locate verses that might address it with truth. This will lead you to a starting place in terms of verses. As you look them up, ask God to guide you to truth that is specifically for your situation. It is really fun to work with Him in this way. Begin a list of verses below.

Take care not to carelessly "cherry pick" verses, however. Recall our lessons about context in the very first lesson. It is always important to rightly handle the word of truth (2 Timothy 2:15). As I replace lies with God's truth, I want to be sure I am really listening and learning well. This is one aspect of why the Body of Christ in the life of a Christian is so important. Within the Body, we can find other believers who help us discern how God is working in our lives. Within the Body, we find encouragement and accountability. God designed us to live in community.

A second facet of this last practice is to receive God's grace and healing. I often pray a simple prayer inviting God's healing into the places where He has revealed my sin or idolatry. As I "put off" sin, I ask the Holy Spirit to come to those wounded places with healing. Ask for His comfort, His clarity, and His encouragement as you trust and rest in Him.

Chapter Five Prayer and Promise

In the last five lessons we encountered truth and tools about idols and obstacles: how to identify and to reject them. To return to *The Princess and the Pea* metaphor, an idol can be thought of as a "pea" that is hiding in the "mattresses" of your life. The practices below are tools to help you recognize and reject obstacles to intimacy with God. The process can help you get the "peas" out so you can rest in deeper relationship with Him.

- Pray for sensitivity
- Pay attention to pain points
- Present for insight
- Put off and reject lies
- Put on truth and embrace grace

These tools are neither an "instant fix" or a "formula," but practices drawn from the Word to create an environment for spiritual maturation. Sanctification is the Spirit's work; we must cooperate with Him. These practices strengthen that cooperation, but the timing and the terrain He takes you through is all up to Him.

In *The Princess and the Pea*, the princess was honest about something in her bed that kept her from sleeping well. She didn't gloss over a poor night's sleep out of fear of offending her hosts. Uncovering "peas" requires willingness to be honest and vulnerable. It may feel risky, but there is great reward. You can reject obstacles to intimacy with God.

Key Practice: You probably have a sense of areas to which the Holy Spirit is directing your attention. Gathering verses that speak truth to the "peas in your mattress" is a great start. Ask God to guide you to one verse to study and meditate on. Work on memorizing it as well.

Key Promise: "So Jesus said to the Jews who had believed him, 'If you abide in my word, you are truly my disciples, and you will know the truth and the truth will set you free.'"

John 8:31-32 (ESV)

Father, your grace is so wide and high and deep. Thank you that there is nothing in my life hidden from you. I ask you to help me know you more fearlessly and more intimately. Give me the courage to be honest as I seek to uncover obstacles that rob me of resting in you and your love for me.

Notes

Notes

Chapter Six: Rest in Relationship

Key Idea: You can rest in an intimate relationship with God.

Key Verse: "Then Jesus said, 'Come to me, all of you who are weary and carry heavy burdens, and I will give you rest. Take my yoke upon you. Let me teach you, because I am humble and gentle at heart, and you will find rest for your souls. For my yoke is easy to bear, and the burden I give you is light."

Matthew 11:28-30 (NLT)

We've covered a lot of ground in the past five chapters, exploring many truths and tools as we've studied. Perhaps you have encountered new truth; perhaps you have been reminded of things you already knew. We all need to reorient ourselves to deeper intimacy with God, because there is no end to the depths of His love. We can always find more of Him!

We focus now on resting in intimate relationship with God. The quest for intimacy and rest in God demands intention. That intentional focus includes learning to be reoriented, learning to receive, and learning the rhythms of life lived in and through Christ. Learning to live in God's power is at the heart of why we study the Word of God in the first place. To know Him. To enjoy Him. To know we are seen and adored. To lean "the unforced rhythms of grace" (Matthew 11:29 MSG).

As you've studied Isaiah 30, you have seen God wooing you with an invitation to rest in Him regardless of circumstances. He invites you to recover your identity and to increase your intimacy with Him. He longs to show you how to increase your sensitivity to His voice and to the voices that seek to pull you away from Him. We finish this last chapter of study both exploring a few more new things and reaching back to truths we have learned in the past lessons.

Lesson One: Rest is the Quest

O loving God, Jesus, Holy Spirit, come into my time of study today. Give me eyes to see and ears to hear what you desire to show me in your Word.

Time for Another Breakup?

Isaiah 30 reveals God's deep commitment to pursue His children and to draw them into life-giving reliance upon Him. We've seen God both warning and wooing His wayward children. One of the ways God pursues is through asking us to leave behind our idols, to give up alliances with things like Egypt that "bring neither help nor profit, but shame and disgrace" (Isaiah 30:5).

Our study has centered on our loving Father's invitation to rest in Him in an intimate relationship characterized by His grace, His nearness, and His direction. But He is a jealous God (Exodus 20:5). The quest for resting in Him demands intentional, singular focus.

Once upon a time, God asked me to break up with Wonder Woman and choose Him more fully instead. As you quest for restful intimacy with God, it's time to consider another breakup. You need to break up with the idea that you can have a problem-free life.

The temptation to seek a problem-free life is sneaky. It challenges us at every turn. The loud voices of our world constantly shout at us. The lens of our flesh says, "that sounds like a GREAT idea." The enemy's lies whisper, "problem-free living is an attainable goal." But if you chase a problem-free life, you are chasing something never to be fulfilled on this earth. It is a delight reserved for Heaven. Jesus says, "In this world you will have trouble. But take heart! I have overcome the world" (John 16:33b NIV).

Read Isaiah 30:20. What circumstances does the first half of this verse mention?

Read the verses below, noting what each one reveals of the Bible's perspective on a problem-free life. Record information you find about the purpose of trials or suffering.

Luke 6:22-23

Romans 8:16-18

2 Corinthians 12:9-10

James 1:2-4

1 Peter 1:6-7

Write a summary of what you've learned about the Bible's perspective on trials. How is this different from the messages of the world around you?

The quest for a problem-free life is an idol. It is another *P* in the mattress that will steal as much of your rest as it can. As a princess in the Kingdom of God, you cannot afford to be swayed by a quest for this false hope. If this is an area of struggle for you, utilize the practices you learned in the last chapter to bring this issue before the Lord.

Return to Your Invitation

In our family, important invitations get put on the refrigerator for all to see. God's invitation in Isaiah 30:15 is one worth keeping front and center, especially for gaining perspective on challenges in our lives. Write the verse below, from memory if you can.

We were created for union with God, for walking in intimacy with Him in the cool of the Garden of Eden (Genesis 3). Though sin and disobedience marred that intimacy, Jesus has purchased the way back for us on the cross. Intimacy with God empowers us to rest in situations that might otherwise cause us to run. It fuels us with strength; it offers salvation from the threats that, at times, surround us. We will not have a problem-free life, but we can have a vibrant and restful life as we clothe ourselves with Christ.

In Chapter Three you studied verses containing the Greek phrase *en Christos*. This phrase indicates an "ingrafting with Christ, in fellowship and union with Christ."[30]

Go back to pages 52-53 and review things you learned about what is yours as you live in Christ. Look also at the chart on pages 55-56 comparing orphan experiences with daughter experiences. As you reconnect with these truths about your identity, choose one or two that are especially significant to you. Why do these stand out to you right now?

With all that is yours in Christ, you have ample resources for rest available, even for life in this problem-filled world. Through union with Christ, you can find rest for your soul regardless of your circumstances.

Read Romans 8:35-39. What circumstances can separate you from God's love?

---

[30] "Strong's #1722 - Ἐν - Thayer's Expanded Definition." *StudyLight.org*, www.studylight.org/lexicons/eng/greek/1722.html.

Lesson Two: Reorientation Required

O loving God, Jesus, Holy Spirit, come into my time of study today. Give me eyes to see and ears to hear what you desire to show me in your Word.

Transformation and Transition

One part of developing a more intimate relationship with God is submitting ourselves and our hearts to the work of His reorientation. The Holy Spirit is at work sanctifying believers, conforming us more and more into the image of Christ. As we are transformed by the renewing of our minds (Romans 12:2), we are being reoriented.

Studying Isaiah 30, we've explored different arenas for reorientation, including identity and idolatry. Reorientation involves transition. Transitions, even good ones, can be unsettling because they jumble up things we have come to rely upon. Most people are creatures of habit. We instinctively resist change, even if it is a change for our good.

Ancient Judah was oriented to believe they were on their own, that no help was coming from God. They desperately needed reorientation, but they didn't want it. They had closed their ears to God.

Our Patient, Loving God

As we explored in Chapter Four, Isaiah 30:18 reveals a patient, waiting God. We also noted a shift in narration and tone at this verse. Isaiah 30 has two halves. The word *way* is used once in each half of the chapter. Each use reveals a different type of orientation to God.

Read Isaiah 30:9-11. Notice the word *way* in verse 11. What is its context?

Who is speaking the word *way*?

What sort of relationship with God is depicted here?

Read Isaiah 30:20-21. Notice the word *way* in verse 21. What is its context?

Who is speaking the word *way*?

What sort of relationship with God is depicted here?

The first occurrence of *way* reveals fractured relationship; the second reveals a picture of intimacy. This reflects the overall outline of Isaiah 30—verses 1-17 are oriented around disobedience and its consequences, while verses 18-33 are oriented around what reliance upon God looks like.

The first half is an outline of broken reality; the second half is a picture of victorious intimacy, of hope, and of opportunity. What must happen to get from one place to the other? Surrender.

The Way of Surrender

Our hearts, like Judah's, are bent toward being our own masters. We are called to bend them to the Lord. We need to allow the Holy Spirit to reorient us, because at the heart of intimacy with God is surrender to His love and His leadership.

Read Romans 12:2. What is the first instruction given?

Describe your thoughts about the spirit of our world or the spirit of our age.

Surrendering is countercultural. Most people like to think they are in charge. Surrender is the way of return, of rest, of quiet confidence, and of trust in God. It is the way of salvation and strength. It is also the proper order of things. Read the verses below and note what they reveal about who we are and who God is.

Isaiah 64:8

Ephesians 2:8-10

We are His workmanship. It isn't the other way around. The spirit of our age, however, declares man to be the measure of all things. It tells us we should live our own truths, show up for ourselves, and win at all costs, among other bad advice. Romans 12:2 exhorts us not to conform to those patterns. It tells us to be reoriented.

The Way of Grace

One obstacle to surrender and reorientation is that we can have a decent amount of success in our own strength. Those successes can tempt us to boast and to think we don't need any help. Ephesians 2:8-9 reveals that God's way is the way of grace so that no man can boast. He doesn't want me to be tripped up into thinking that I can manage things on my own. Why?

Because we aren't made to carry the weight of the world.

God offers us gifts of grace and faith so we can rest in His sufficiency. He does this because He loves us and knows what wars against us. He doesn't want us to feel the burden of managing things in our own strength for even a moment. It's a grace to be reoriented to weaknesses.

If I am tempted to do things myself, I am snared into a whole host of traps. One of the biggest is the trap of pride. Read James 4:4-8 and answer the questions below.

What does this passage say about pride?

What does it say about grace?

How does it describe friendship with the world?

What do you see in the passage related to the world's loud voices, the lenses of our flesh, and/or the enemy's lies?

This chapter began with a challenge to break up with the idea that you can have a problem-free life. It is one example of where reorientation from the loud voices and lies of the world is needed. Surrendering to the Holy Spirit's transforming work helps us see our lives through the lens of God's ways and not the world's ways.

James 4:4-8 draws a stark contrast between these two ways, just as there is a stark contrast between the two contexts of the word *way* in Isaiah 30.

Read John 14:6. What is the way mentioned here?

According to this verse, what else does He offer?

Lesson Three: Receiving Means Risk

O loving God, Jesus, Holy Spirit, come into my time of study today. Give me eyes to see and ears to hear what you desire to show me in your Word.

Release to Receive

As we surrender to God and His riches, as we give away self, idols, and false identity, we are opened into a place of receiving. We empty in order to be filled. We are invited to experience more of Him. The question is: Are you willing to receive? Or do you hesitate at the entrance to the path to more of Him?

Why wouldn't we want to receive more of God? For one thing, we like our familiar comfort. Intimacy requires transition and reorientation. This pushes us out of our comfort zones. We may also struggle to receive God's gift of intimacy because of risk aversion or fear. Surrender feels like a risk. It requires a deep trust in the one we surrender to. That vulnerability can be very hard.

It is even harder, perhaps, to admit we are like Judah, unsure we can trust God. In the first lesson of this study, we looked at the types of threats and intimidation Assyria used to strike fear into Judah. Go back to pages 2-4 and look at the subheadings. Write out the third, fourth, and fifth ones below.

We also have an enemy who whispers lies into our ears about how dangerous it is to surrender to God. What you wrote above are just some of the tactics the enemy likes to use. He wants us to believe our obstacles are too big, too messy, or too far gone for God to have anything to do with. The enemy of our souls wants us to live in fear.

He certainly doesn't want us to become more surrendered to God.

"But There are Risks"

Imagine yourself in the place of the ancient Judeans. The Assyrians have destroyed neighboring nations, and masses of people have been killed or taken away into captivity. Now they are headed your way. Your army is no match, so you turn to a regional superpower—Egypt. Finally, a military alliance that might protect your home and your family from being slaughtered or captured by Assyria!

Into this scenario God says: "You've made a bad agreement. It won't profit you. Come to me. I will give you salvation and strength. But you must break the alliance with Egypt. You must trust me completely."

What are the first feelings you have as you place yourself in the spot of Judah hearing God's invitation? Is it excitement? Is it fear? Is it doubt? Or something else? Write your response below.

Your reactions will give insight into your thoughts about surrendering to the Holy Spirit. If your reactions are more on the fearful or doubtful side, talk with the Lord about it. He is so very gentle with our hearts.

At times, I have been so stuck in a place of fear that the best prayer I could come up with was: *Lord, I am not sure I am willing to do this. But I am willing to be made willing. So come and meet me there.* If that sounds like where you are right now, take heart. He can work with that. Jesus once said something encouraging about faith the size of a mustard seed (Matthew 17:20).

Stopping At the Edge of the Cliff

I voice-text notes and reminders to myself. I discovered a funny thing about autocorrect while writing this Bible study. Every time I said the word *intimacy*, autocorrect spelled it *into-the-sea.*

That sounds familiar to me. As you can imagine after hearing some of my story, I have battled trust issues over the years. Intimacy sounded a lot like being asked to dive "into the sea." I heard His invitations to intimacy and to more of Him. I longed deeply for the joys and freedoms I saw in other people. My trust issues were deeper. Following God often felt like being asked to jump into the sea from the edge of a very high cliff.

To receive more intimacy with God, we must release what stands between us and Him. For me, that release often feels incredibly risky; I fall on the high end of the risk-aversion scale. There can be paralysis for me at the edge of the intimacy cliff. But, oh, the love of God! He has been so tender and gracious; He has been so patient. He reminds me that feelings aren't reality, that I am completely safe in His care, and that His power in both the seen and unseen realms is unrivaled. He holds my hand as I surrender fears to Him, making room in my heart for more trust in Him. I want you to know, friend, how very trustworthy my broken and battered heart has found Him to be.

Sometimes the path from the *here* of our circumstances to the *there* of intimacy with God feels as if it requires stepping off the edge of a high cliff overlooking an angry, stormy sea churning against enormous rocks.

What allows us to take that first step? Our faith in Christ. Even if it is mustard seed sized. Jesus can speak "Peace! Be Still!" to all the churning waves. He's done it before.

Jesus Speaks "Peace! Be Still!"

Read Mark 4:35-41. What does this show about faith and God's willingness to act?

Read Mark 9:20-24. What do you learn about faith here?

Read Luke 17:5-6. What do the disciples ask Jesus for?

Read 2 Thessalonians 1:3. What does this teach about faith?

God gives peace even when our faith isn't strong; He heals when our belief is only a fraction of what we'd like it to be. Our faith can grow, and we can pray for more faith.

Like the disciples panicking in the boat then being stunned by the power of Jesus, you can learn not to be shut down or stuck by your pain points. They are an opportunity to praise God for giving you the chance to practice more trust. They are the places where we find our desperation for Him.

It's not a bad thing to be desperate for God. The Psalms speak of this often. Psalm 84 is a beautiful poem speaking of longing for God, as well as the blessing of finding your strength in Him. Read it and make notes of phrases that stand out to you.

Close your time now talking with God about your risk tolerance and ways you may have held back a willingness to surrender to Him. Ask Him to increase your faith and trust in Him.

Lesson Four: Rhythm of Relationship

O loving God, Jesus, Holy Spirit, come into my time of study today. Give me eyes to see and ears to hear what you desire to show me in your Word.

Significant Commitment

The story of the Bible is the story of God. In His story, we see He has a significant commitment to His children, pursuing them through generations, sacrificing His only Son, inviting them to intimate, eternal fellowship with Him.

Intimacy with God also requires significant commitment on our part. We've been looking at that in this last chapter. You've been asked to break up with the idea of a problem-free life, to be reoriented to God's ways of grace and surrender, and to consider honestly whether risk aversion undercuts what God wants to do in your life. The only way to rest in intimacy with Him is to allow Him to cut away the parts of us that stand in the way. Otherwise, we are unwittingly fighting against the relationship.

Read John 15:1-2. Who is speaking?

What is the relationship between pruning and fruitfulness?

Reflect on the past three lessons about trials, reorientation, and risk. What has the Lord been revealing to you that might require pruning out of your life?

God will want to work with you on whatever He is identifying as you deepen your relationship with Him. The places we need pruning are part of the rhythm of the intimate relationship with Him we are invited into.

Relationship: Abide

Let's continue with Jesus' gardening metaphor in John 15. As you read the passage below circle words describing the relationship He offers.

> Live in me. Make your home in me just as I do in you. In the same way that a
>
> branch can't bear grapes by itself but only by being joined to the vine, you can't
>
> bear fruit unless you are joined with me. I am the Vine, you are the branches.
>
> When you're joined with me and I with you, the relation intimate and organic,
>
> the harvest is sure to be abundant. Separated, you can't produce a thing.
>
> (John 15:4-5 MSG)

Did you notice the word *intimate* in this translation? What does this passage say about producing fruit?

Read Galatians 5:22. What is the fruit described here? List it below.

According to John 15:4-5, how is this fruit produced?

The only way to enjoy the abundant life Jesus came to provide us (John 10:10) is by abiding in Him. He tends our hearts with the care of a nurturing gardener working to produce a bountiful harvest.

Relationship: Rhythms

Each chapter of this study has a title. The first word of each title is an imperative, which is the verb form used to give instruction or a command. The next word or phrase tells what to direct the action of the verb toward. The title of Chapter One is *Recognize Circumstances*. The instruction is to recognize something, and the thing to recognize is circumstances.

Go back and find the title of each chapter and write them in order below.

What do these imperative phrases have in common? They are all aspects of an intimate relationship with God gleaned from studying Isaiah 30. They are paths through which your relationship with God can flow. Each of those actions are things He asks you to do. Interestingly, each is also something for which you can ask God's direction. They are arenas for prayer, for growth, for fellowship, and for conversation with Him.

Within the list above, like a smaller matryoshka doll nested inside a larger one, is the process you learned about in Chapter Five. Go back to page 106 and find the bullet-pointed list summarizing the chapter. Write it below.

This second list is a process of developing discernment to identify and reject obstacles to intimacy with God. This list helps you reject idols, recover your identity, and respond more fully to God's invitation to intimacy.

There are similarities in the two lists you've just made. Rather than a formula, there is fluidity within the ways God will guide you through these actions. They are channels through which God wants to relate to you and in which He invites you to relate to Him. Together, these lists offer practices that form a rhythm of intimate relationship with God.

Like musical rhythms, relational rhythms with God are to be repeated. Musically speaking, a rhythm is an established, repeated pulse underpinning a piece of music. Spiritually speaking, relational rhythms form a heartbeat in your relationship with God, bringing vitality and life.

Read 2 Corinthians 3:18. According to this verse, what is happening to believers?

Who is doing this transformation?

Does this transformation happen all at once? If not, how does it happen?

From one degree of glory to another, our hearts can beat in rhythm with our Father's heart. We are being drawn ever deeper into His likeness through the purifying work of the Spirit of God within us.

Relationship: Rest

In music, rhythm also serves to create unity and coherence, tying together other elements in a piece. Because rhythm establishes a sense of timing, it gives the listener something to follow. There is an inviting steadiness in that foundation.

Spiritually speaking, our steady foundation is Christ. He brings unity and coherence. Intimate relationship with Him establishes a sense of timing in our lives which brings security and restfulness as we follow the rhythms He establishes. Jesus invites us to live in rhythm with Him.

> Are you tired? Worn out? Burned out on religion? Come to me. Get away with me and you'll recover your life. I'll show you how to take a real rest. Walk with me and work with me—watch how I do it. Learn the unforced rhythms of grace. I won't lay anything heavy or ill-fitting on you. Keep company with me and you'll learn to live freely and lightly. (Matthew 11:28-30 MSG)

According to this passage, what sort of rhythms can we learn as we follow Jesus?

How do we learn to rest?

How do we learn to live freely and lightly?

Lesson Five: Rejoice and Reflect

O loving God, Jesus, Holy Spirit, come into my time of study today. Give me eyes to see and ears to hear what you desire to show me in your Word.

Rejoice: He Does the Heavy Lifting

We have studied many things over the last six chapters. Somewhere along the line, I imagine God has invited you to consider entering places that may not feel comfortable. Maybe responding to invitation, recovering identity, rejecting idols, or some other facet of this study has left you feeling this invitation to intimacy is more than you can handle. My prayer for you is a blessing found in one of my favorite verses:

> May the God of hope fill you with all joy and peace in believing, so that by the power of the Holy Spirit you may abound in hope. (Romans 15:13 ESV)

I like this verse because it paints a picture of God doing the heavy lifting.

Rejoice: He Completes

Relationship with God, like any other relationship, will have its own ups and downs. When we are in a down cycle, it is tempting to believe we have failed and things will never get better. Guess what? God is on top of things even when you aren't.

Read Philippians 1:6. What does it tell you about your journey of sanctification?

Reflect: Looking Back and Ahead

Now that you are armed with the hope and assurance that God will complete the good work He has begun in you, reflect on what you have learned through this study. You may need to go back and look at your notes from previous lessons. Take your time and linger with Him over the questions below.

Review the things you've assessed and learned. The truths. The tools. What are your three biggest takeaways?

What are two promises from His Word you will carry forward? Consider writing them out and posting them somewhere you see frequently or creating a graphic to print or to use as a lock screen for your phone.

What is one practice from this study God is leading you to bring into your life regularly?

Another Old Testament prophet, Jeremiah, shared this instruction from the Lord:

> Thus says the LORD: "Stand by the roads, and look, and ask for the ancient paths, where the good way is; and walk in it, and find rest for your souls. But they said, 'We will not walk in it'" Jeremiah 6:16 (ESV).

You might notice the last sentence of this verse is chillingly familiar. A similar phrase appears at the end of the invitation of God in Isaiah 30:15. Jeremiah also ministered to the nation of Judah, nearly a century after Isaiah. Still God's people were refusing Him.

Another thing Isaiah 30:15 and Jeremiah 6:16 have in common is an invitation to rest. God invites us to rest. He repeatedly did so in ancient times; He continues to do so today.

During this study, we have done a good bit of "asking for the ancient paths." We went to words more than 2,500 years old and found an invitation and promises that haven't changed in all the years since.

Let us have one change, though.

Let us change our response from those recorded in Isaiah 30:15 and Jeremiah 6:16. Let us return, rest, trust, have quiet confidence, and walk in the good way. Let us find rest for our souls in Him and Him alone.

Key Promise: "The steadfast love of the LORD never ceases; his mercies never come to an end; they are new every morning; great is your faithfulness."

Lamentations 3:22-23 (ESV)

Father, thank you for your faithfulness generation after generation. Thank you that your character never changes, your steadfast love never ceases, and that you are merciful forever. May I rest in you. May I find more than I could have asked or imagined in intimate, ever-deepening relationship with you, my loving Father.

Notes

Appendix

Isaiah 30 (ESV)

[1] "Ah, stubborn children," declares the LORD, "who carry out a plan, but not mine, and who make an alliance, but not of my Spirit, that they may add sin to sin; [2] who set out to go down to Egypt, without asking for my direction, to take refuge in the protection of Pharaoh and to seek shelter in the shadow of Egypt! [3] Therefore shall the protection of Pharaoh turn to your shame, and the shelter in the shadow of Egypt to your humiliation. [4] For though his officials are at Zoan and his envoys reach Hanes, [5] everyone comes to shame through a people that cannot profit them, that brings neither help nor profit, but shame and disgrace."

[6] An oracle on the beasts of the Negeb. Through a land of trouble and anguish, from where come the lioness and the lion, the adder and the flying fiery serpent, they carry their riches on the backs of donkeys, and their treasures on the humps of camels, to a people that cannot profit them. [7] Egypt's help is worthless and empty; therefore I have called her "Rahab who sits still."

A Rebellious People

[8] And now, go, write it before them on a tablet and inscribe it in a book, that it may be for the time to come as a witness forever. [9] For they are a rebellious people, lying children, children unwilling to hear the instruction of the LORD; [10] who say to the seers, "Do not see," and to the prophets, "Do not prophesy to us what is right; speak to us smooth things, prophesy illusions, [11] leave the way, turn aside from the path, let us hear no more about the Holy One of Israel."

[12] Therefore thus says the Holy One of Israel, "Because you despise this word and trust in oppression and perverseness and rely on them, [13] therefore this iniquity shall be to you like a breach in a high wall, bulging out and about to collapse, whose breaking comes suddenly, in an instant; [14] and its breaking is like that of a potter's vessel that is smashed so ruthlessly that among its fragments not a shard is found with which to take fire from the hearth, or to dip up water out of the cistern."

[15] For thus said the Lord GOD, the Holy One of Israel, "In returning and rest you shall be saved; in quietness and in trust shall be your strength." But you were unwilling, [16] and you said, "No! We will flee upon horses"; therefore you shall flee away; and, "We will ride upon

swift steeds"; therefore your pursuers shall be swift. ¹⁷ A thousand shall flee at the threat of one; at the threat of five you shall flee, till you are left like a flagstaff on the top of a mountain, a signal on a hill.

The Lord Will Be Gracious

¹⁸ Therefore the Lord waits to be gracious to you, and therefore he exalts himself to show mercy to you. For the Lord is a God of justice; blessed are all those who wait for him. ¹⁹ For a people shall dwell in Zion, in Jerusalem; you shall weep no more. He will surely be gracious to you at the sound of your cry. As soon as he hears it, he answers you. ²⁰ And though the Lord give you the bread of adversity and the water of affliction, yet your Teacher will not hide himself anymore, but your eyes shall see your Teacher. ²¹ And your ears shall hear a word behind you, saying, "This is the way, walk in it," when you turn to the right or when you turn to the left. ²² Then you will defile your carved idols overlaid with silver and your gold-plated metal images. You will scatter them as unclean things. You will say to them, "Be gone!"

²³ And he will give rain for the seed with which you sow the ground, and bread, the produce of the ground, which will be rich and plenteous. In that day your livestock will graze in large pastures, ²⁴ and the oxen and the donkeys that work the ground will eat seasoned fodder, which has been winnowed with shovel and fork. ²⁵ And on every lofty mountain and every high hill there will be brooks running with water, in the day of the great slaughter, when the towers fall. ²⁶ Moreover, the light of the moon will be as the light of the sun, and the light of the sun will be sevenfold, as the light of seven days, in the day when the Lord binds up the brokenness of his people, and heals the wounds inflicted by his blow.

²⁷ Behold, the name of the Lord comes from afar, burning with his anger, and in thick rising smoke; his lips are full of fury, and his tongue is like a devouring fire; ²⁸ his breath is like an overflowing stream that reaches up to the neck; to sift the nations with the sieve of destruction, and to place on the jaws of the peoples a bridle that leads astray.

²⁹ You shall have a song as in the night when a holy feast is kept, and gladness of heart, as when one sets out to the sound of the flute to go to the mountain of the Lord, to the Rock of Israel. ³⁰ And the Lord will cause his majestic voice to be heard and the descending blow of his arm to be seen, in furious anger and a flame of devouring fire, with a cloudburst and storm and hailstones. ³¹ The Assyrians will be terror-stricken at the voice of the Lord, when he strikes with his rod. ³² And every stroke of the appointed staff that the Lord lays on them will be to the sound of tambourines and lyres. Battling with brandished arm, he will fight with them. ³³ For a burning place has long been prepared; indeed, for the king it is made ready, its pyre made deep and wide, with fire and wood in abundance; the breath of the Lord, like a stream of sulfur, kindles it.

About the Author

Elizabeth Renicks is a Bible teacher, writer, and speaker. More than that, she is a woman who knows the beauty of discovering real intimacy with God after exhausting years of striving in her own strength. With warmth, wisdom, and a deep love for Scripture, she equips women to foster a restful, restorative relationship with Christ.

Elizabeth lives in Alabama with her husband and their two sons. An avid reader and lifelong learner, she ministers through teaching and discipleship in her church and local homeschool community. Find her at elizabethrenicks.com.

What Could Your Life Look Like with More of Him?

Twice a month, I send grace-filled encouragement straight to your inbox to help you slow down and reconnect with God.

The *More of Him* newsletter includes:

- Encouragement to quiet the noise and hear God's voice
- Simple reminders of truth, identity, and grace
- Scripture-based prompts to keep you grounded and growing

Subscribe below and let's walk toward *more of Him—* together.

THANK YOU GIFT:
A free PDF copy of a 10-day devotional:
Truths About God's Guidance

ELIZABETH RENICKS

Find even more resources for increasing your intimacy with Him at
www.elizabethrenicks.com

* 9 7 9 8 9 9 9 9 4 3 5 4 0 8 *